Pre-emptive strikes
for
Winning fights

'The alternative to grappling'

by
Jamie O'Keefe

Reprinted in Aug 2001 (7th edition)

Printed by
New Breed Publishing
Po box 511
Dagenham
Essex RM9 5DN

New Breed Publishing
Po Box 511
Dagenham
Essex RM9 5DN

Email: books@newbreed.worldonline.co.uk

Web Site: www.newbreedbooks.co.uk

Copyright Jamie O'Keefe 1998©

Published by

New Breed publishing 1998

No part of this book may be reproduced by any means, nor transmitted, nor translated into machine language, without the written permission of the publisher.

A CIP catalogue record for this book is available from the British Library

Printed and bound in Great Britain.

ISBN 0 9517567 3 7

Dedicated to Darrel Bent (who is fighting MS)
and all others that have found,
or are seeking the courage to
'Fight back'
It is these special individuals who put
everything else that we consider to be
problems, into perspective.
Darrel my thoughts are with you.

Jamie

Acknowledgements

Thanks to: -

Everyone at New Breed for support.

Steve Kemp and Micky Neale for giving up their Saturday morning to help me with the photographs.

Pete Chamberlain for photographs.

Steve and Vicky for proof reading.

Pam King for 'Grappling painting' of

Steve Kemp and Brian Flint

at the New Breed Academy

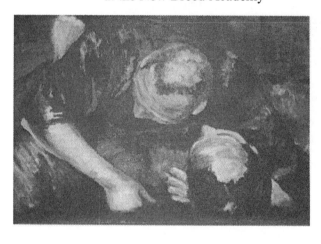

Painted by Pam King

About the Author

Jamie O'Keefe has spent 25 years studying, training and teaching the Martial Arts. He presently holds the rank of 6th Dan black belt with the Self Defence Federation and is the chief instructor of his own 'New Breed system of Self Protection.' Additionally he is also a former bouncer and spent his last 15-years prior to becoming an author, working the door. Whilst working as a doorman Jamie studied and gained his City & Guilds 'Further and Adult Education Teachers Certificate' and then his Cert ed. 'Certificate in Education and training' from Greenwich University. He is also a 'Founder fellow of the Society of Martial Arts, (F.S.M.A.) and is an NVQ D32 D33 Assessor.

In 1999 Jamie was also awarded a place and entered into 'Combat' magazines very first martial arts 'Hall of Fame' in recognition of his 25 years of commitment and devotion to the development of Martial Arts in the United Kingdom and around the world.

Jamie has written many articles for Martial Arts magazines and is a former columnist for 'Martial Arts Illustrated' and now writes for 'Combat' magazine. He has also appeared on BBC radio and on Television as an authority on Self-protection and was booked as the Self Protection coach for Seni 2000 and Senni 2001 at the Birmingham Exhibition centre. This is his fifth book on Self Protection related subjects.

Jamie's other books are:

Dogs don't know kung fu - *A guide to female self-protection*
Old School-New School – *The only bouncers training guide*
What makes tough guys tough – *How to become tougher*
Thugs, Mugs, and Violence – *Jamie's autobiography*
No One Fears When Angry – *Psychology of confrontation*

CONTENTS

TECHNIQUES

18. Headbutt
19. Bite
20. Shoulder-butt
21. Elbow
22. Forearm
23. Wrist to Clavicle
24. Knifehand
25. Chop
26. Backhand slap
27. Innerhand slap
28. Palm strike
29. Backfist
30. Hammerfist
31. Club punch
32. Jab

TECHNIQUES

33. Cross
34. Hook
35. Uppercut
36. Finger jab
37. Arc hand to throat
38. Windpipe squeeze
39. Hair grab
40. Head twist
41. Knee
42. Rising kicks
43. Round kicks
44. Thrust forward kicks
45. Thrust backward kicks
46. Stamping kicks
47. Death stare – visual strike
48. Verbal attack psycho strike
49. Weapon strikes

* All techniques displayed with in this book, both empty-handed and with weapons, have been taken directly from Jamie O'Keefe's 'New Breed Self Protection System.'

THEORY CONTINUED

Foreword

On first meeting Jamie O'Keefe, I was struck by his warmth and humour. I was then struck by his fists, head, & knees... Having been on the receiving end (though thankfully only in training) I can attest to the extreme effectiveness of the techniques he teaches. However, as I got to know him better, I was even more impressed by his integrity, honesty and commitment to teaching. Like many of the finest instructors and toughest fighters, Jamie is a gentleman.

These days I consider Jamie a good friend, but that's not why I agreed to write this forward. I believe he writes some of the best material available on modern self-protection, material, which can be, quite literally, life saving.
I am proud to be able to associate my name with such valuable work

So what is the value in devoting a whole book to the pre-emptive strike?

Be in no doubt that this is one of the most important concepts for personal protection you will ever learn. Over the years I have read about, trained with and worked the door with many individuals who have vast experience of real violence. Every single one of them *without exception* recommends and uses the pre-emptive strike as the prime tactic for self-protection when a physical assault seems inevitable.

This book thoroughly dissects the theory, training and practical application of the pre-emptive strategy. From legal and moral ramifications to pre-attack indicators, from action triggers to Jamie's unique 'Strike Storage & Retrieval System', this book is the most exhaustive, insightful and thought-provoking treatise on the subject I have yet seen.

The lessons contained within these pages were learned the hard way, with spilt, blood & broken bones - this book was written so you don't have to take that route.

Read, absorb, and live by Jamie's advice. You'll be stronger and safer for it.

When talk fails and escape is impossible or impractical, the pre-emptive strike is your best option. I'll let Jamie tell you why.

Simon James
Instructor, Close Quarter Combat Systems

The Simon James full-length interview with Jamie can be found in December 2000 and January 2001 issues of 'Combat Magazine'

Introduction

There is a great misunderstanding in today's society that attacking first to protect yourself is wrong; and that you have to wait until you are attacked before you are allowed to protect yourself.

Unfortunately this misinformation comes to us via the people that we trust most of all to give us accurate and up to date information. Those educators are the police, lawyers, and even your own martial arts instructors who should play the main role in teaching and educating you about self-protection.

I think that there are two main reasons that you are being misinformed as to your legal position within self-protection. One being that most people are unaware of how and when you are allowed to strike first in order to protect yourself. Secondly, some of those people that are aware of it; choose not to make this information freely available through fear of it being abused, which I will discuss in detail later in the book.

The only time we normally come across the term 'Pre-emptive strike' is when we hear people talking of war and methods of attack using military aircraft, submarines or ships to attack. However at street level when discussing a possible single or multiple threat of attack, we never seem to use the concept of pre-emptive strike. This is why I have written this book in order to bring home to you the concept of the pre-emptive strike.

The techniques in this book are to serve as a secondary guide just to aid those of you that want something visual to link to the concept, in order to give you a clearer understanding of the pre-emptive strike. I do not like or write technique books. I find them boring and feel they are not the best format or method of teaching techniques. Video is an excellent medium for teaching techniques, which is secondary to a real tutor. So please do not flick through the book going '*I know that technique, and that one, and that one*' because in doing so you will be missing the point! This is not a technique book.

The message I am trying to get across to you is the concept of the pre-emptive strike along with the Why? Where? and when to use it?

How? Is up to you. I have included many different types of pre-emptive strikes just to give you an idea as to types of strike if you are 'new' to the fighting arts. However, for those of you that are already involved in an art and are proficient at striking, use your own methods of striking. All you have to do is learn and remember to use it pre-emptively.

I do not want to criticise, compare, or challenge your current system of training. I want to enhance, promote and show you that you probably already have '*Pre-emptive strikes for winning fights*' but just need to use them pre-emptively rather than them just being shelved weapons that you know can be used in a fight, as and when you are able.

I want to change your thinking and outlook towards understanding that you **can** legally strike the first blow to protect yourself if you '*fear for your safety.*'

If you do not currently train in a fighting art and need further material to aid you in your studies towards self protection, I am soon to release a video on '*Pre-emptive strikes for winning fights*' which will give you the techniques in this book plus much more. Everybody on the New Breed database will automatically informed when this video is available.

The Law

'The law states that if the antagonist is aggressive and moving forward, and you fear for your safety, you can legally pre-emptively strike the first blow in self defence'

Lets break this down into understandable terms so that we all understand what it is that they are saying.

Law = The law of the land by which we are governed by.
Antagonist = Enemy, Foe, Opponent, Opposition, Rivalry.
Aggressive = Combative, Warlike, Hostile, Offensive.
Moving forward = Towards you or an item dangerous to you.
Fear = Fright, Terror, Dread, Apprehension.
Safety = Security, Protection, Invulnerability, Sanctuary.
Legally = Within the law.
Pre-emptively = Make the first move before your opponent does, in order to prevent their intended attack carrying on.

Technically the antagonist does not even have to be moving towards you because his actions may cause you to fear for your safety in another way. For example he could be walking towards a weapon that you believe he is going to harm you with. The most important thing that you need to remember is that you 'Feared for your safety.' **Only** when this condition is present can you perform your pre-emptive strike and then **only** in Self-defence. So the running order is:

1. Aggressive opponent
2. You fear for your safety
3. You strike pre-emptively

The pre-emptive strike can quite easily be abused by someone with knowledge of the correct running order as above because technically you could claim that anyone that comes near you looking aggressive in any way, made you fear for your safety, so you hit then pre-emptively in self defence!

What is a Pre-emptive Strike?

To make this as simple to understand as possible; I will not as with all my books, colour the explanation with words that will send you off searching for a dictionary and Thesaurus. I want your reading to be easy, understandable and enjoyable.

'To hit somebody prior to allowing them to attack you first is known as a Pre-emptive strike.'

Example:
A guy who asks me for my wallet approaches me. By his actions and omissions I begin to **fear for my safety**. I believe that I am about to become a victim of physical violence. As a response I launch a pre-emptive strike; that being a forceful punch to the guys jaw, knocking him down. I used force in self-defence without anybody physically touching me.

My reasons for doing so were that I **feared for my safety** which in effect means that the guys had committed a *'common assault.'* I launched my attack as a law-abiding citizen to prevent my attacker further engaging in breaking the law.

'No system of law can prevent a state (or, indeed, an individual) from using force in self-defence.'
Encyclopaedia Britannica 1994-1998

Do you see how much easier it is to defend yourself with a little understanding of the law, pre-emptive strike, and how to explain your actions after an event.

What you say and the way in which you explain your reasons for launching a pre-emptive strike are very important after the encounter. I cannot stress how important it is to remember the fact that you 'feared for your safety' before you launched your pre-emptive strike.

The Wasp Analogy

Here is a simple analogy,

A wasp flies near you. Naturally, you fear you are about to be stung. In effect, the wasp has committed a Common Assault.

 Without thinking any more about it you launch your Pre-emptive strike. You are acting in self-defence.
You do not wait to be stung first before swatting the wasp.

I have not really taught you anything new here, have I?

Hopefully, I have just increased your awareness that what applies to wasps also applies to other attackers.
You do not have to wait until you are physically attacked.

However, **you must try to stay within the Law.**

For instance bad doormen and villains could quite easily abuse this legal knowledge and become the aggressor, making out to be in fear of their safety.

The Pre-emptive strike is there to be used and not abused!

<u>If you do **not** genuinely fear for your safety, you are **not** in a legal position to strike first.</u>

Your Defence Must Be Reasonable

I am generally a passive, laid back introvert. I prefer to avoid physical confrontations whenever I can, hoping to settle problems through discussion and verbal dissuasion.
Sadly, some people take my discussion approach as a sign of weakness and proceed to try physical application to get their point across.
This attitude really pisses me off!
I hate it when someone forces me along the path of violence.
They force my preference to change.

If the situation does deteriorate into violence, I always try to remind myself of the possible consequences. That being that we could both be taking a trip in a police van, ambulance or hearse, all because some bully mistook me for an easy target, a weak individual.
So, what do I do?
This guy is seriously pushing his luck. I am sure I can deal with the situation (otherwise I would be attempting to run the four-minute mile by now!)
I am now pissed off with the fighting ability capable of taking a life, without using weapons, very quickly.
If he grabs me I could break his grip, destroy his attack and then proceed to discipline him like he would never forget.
I know what I am capable of. He would end up pulverised and I

would become the 'have a go hero.' Right?
No! Wrong!
The reality is, I could find myself with a **Grievous Bodily Harm** case against me and a free ride in a police car to the station.
Where did I go wrong? *'I was only defending myself, officer!'*

Well! The Law states that

'It is both good Law and good sense that a person who is attacked may defend themselves but that in doing so, they may only do what is reasonably necessary.'

You can rightfully defend yourself but **nothing more**.
No returning the attack with added interest. No breaking your attacker's arms and legs and biting his nose off because he made a threat. The Law is quite clear on the matter.
You may only respond with a self-defence technique, that right-minded people would accept as reasonable, according to the type of attack.
If you were to grab me with the obvious intention of harming me and I retaliated by punching you on the chin, most people would accept that I had acted reasonably.
However, if I proceeded to stamp on your head when you fell to the floor, I would be using excessive and unnecessary force.

Here is the Deal

I see a person moving towards me making threatening remarks and gestures.
I assess the situation and evaluate my options. If I cannot avoid the confrontation and I am in 'fear for my safety.' I can launch my 'Pre-emptive strike.' However, this is the real world and it is easy to miss the moment.
Maybe I was not switched on when the guy first made his move, so I lost the chance of making a Pre-emptive strike. Shit happens!!
I must still remember to remain inside the Law. I can only do what is reasonable to stop the attack. If I knock the man to the floor I may have a new option, calling the police, getting more help. Or running away.
But if I proceed to jump up and down on him for five minutes I would have overstepped the mark.

The Law can work on a fine line and you must be aware of your responsibilities as well as your rights.

If you find yourself in the position of having to make unavoidable physical contact, you need to be aware of other areas of the law.

You may be dealing with someone for reasons outside of the normal street attack scenario, because they have committed Robbery, Theft, Arson, Burglary, Criminal damage, Assault, etc.. and you are making moves to prevent their intended actions from going any further, but in doing so they have made you fear for your safety so you are going to let go a pre-emptive strike.

However in doing so the Criminal Law act (1967) states that you must restrict yourself to using *'only such force as is reasonable in the circumstances'* and the Police and criminal Evidence act (1984) says you must use the '**minimum force necessary to achieve the objective**.'

So How Hard Do I Hit Them?

Just enough, to stop them from perusing their intention to harm you. Nothing more, nothing less! However this in itself can be very complicated. How do you know that your strike will be sufficient enough to stop the attacker and allow you to get away from this situation?

The law of the land really gives us a rough deal in its interpretation of what we are allowed to do in protecting ourselves; so my answer is to stay within the law but apply another set of rules as well.

'You only have one life to protect, if you get it wrong, you may lose that life.'

Your life means more than breaking the law.

The best way for me to explain this grey area of how hard to hit them is to use an analogy.

If you touch the shell of a boiled egg lightly, you will not cause an effect. If you tap it lightly with a spoon you may cause a crack in its shell. If you hit it hard with the spoon, which is in effect your weapon, you will cause irreversible damage. If you cut the head off! It can never return back to its original condition.

I am not suggesting here that you crack open or cut off the head of every person that makes you fear for your safety. I am merely using the boiled egg analogy to show you that a different level of force be needed according to achieve the end desired effect.

The amount of force that you use with your chosen strike is something that you will have to decide on there and then as each situation arises.

If I simply said hit someone on the chin as hard as you can and that will be fine in the eyes of the law; I would be misinforming you.

For all I know it could be Mike Tyson reading this book and I'm advising him to hit everyone that makes him fear for his safety as hard as he can on the chin!

Look where that got him, another year in prison.

So as you can see there is no hard and fast rules when deciding how hard you should hit somebody but with a little common-sense you should be able to judge it by looking at your attackers body frame, body language, and their actions, as to the amount of force that you are going to need in stopping their intended attack on you going any further.

My own personal set of rules that I use to aid me in my choice as to which level of attack to use is different. As I said earlier; I only have one life to protect and if I get it wrong and underestimate the seriousness of an attack; I may lose that life.

I am not prepared to take that risk just to give my attacker a gentleman's 'Benefit of the doubt' chance.

Anybody that makes me fear for my safety will have a 100% explosive pre-emptive array of stikes to deal with as my way of thanking them for forcing me along the path of violence. I detest violence and hate it even more when forced to use it against my will. As for the law of the land? At least I will still be alive after the encounter to explain my case to the law rather than dead and a victim of the 'Benefit of doubt' gentleman's agreement.

This brings me to your next question.

What Pre-emptive strike should I use?

Well as the old saying goes; **the colour of the cat doesn't matter as long as it catches mice**!

The same applies to your pre-emptive strike! It doesn't matter which one of your bodies' weapons you choose to launch as long as it does the job of stopping the attacker.

Blocks Dont Work

Ok! Here is the section where I begin to lose friends…
Nothing pisses someone off more than when they
have spent years practising to block and I go and lay
claim that they don't work!
Well I'm sorry folks but **action is faster than
reaction**. So get you head out of the sand.
Blocks to me are comparable to a football penalty
shoot out.

As a goalie you are in a prepared stance, are switched on, you're
visually scanning, watching body movement, angle of attack, and
many other factors that you are unaware of such as the strikers
history, reputation, success rate and so on. Another thing to consider
is that the goalie is also
very experienced at
whatever level they are
competing at. Yet goals
still get through and fail
to get blocked.
If you apply these
conditions to a street
attacker who can also

launch the striker style kick along with 1,001 other possible weapons
from unexpected angles and speeds without you having time to
prepare as the goalie can in a penalty shoot out, you will see that
blocks generally, do not work. The nearest you are going to get to a
block working for you is a natural reactional cover-up as if you
suddenly realised that something was going to hit you and you are not
aware of what it is, or where its coming from. This sort of thing
happens in explosions, earthquakes and sudden loud noise situations.

Now the Important Part

If blocks cannot be relied upon, this is all the more reason for striking
pre-emptively because they also will not be ready for it and also will
not know which type of attack you are going to use or what direction
its going to come from.

Most people that do attempt to use a form of block in a sudden attack scenario automatically freeze up and just stand there for a second or two in order to get to grips with what's happening to them.

Please don't make my mistake and rely on blocks to save the day like I did as a young lad; I found out the hard way. Try to accept and understand the weakness of blocking; learn from this book rather than be proved wrong in the street.

Who's Fit Anyway?

Fitness cannot be ignored when it comes to the topic of self-protection, however self defence and the use of pre-emptive strikes should be available for use by anybody regardless of their present level of fitness and health.

What I would like to do here is explain a little about fitness so that you can see what you can, and cannot get away with if you are relying on pre-emptive strikes to win your fights.

Often we make this big promise to ourselves to become fit, but when we say the word 'fit', what exactly do we mean by it? Do we mean lose weight? Do we mean climbing stairs without breathing heavy? Or do we mean running 20 miles today rather than the normal 15 mile run?

I think that for most of us it will be to visually look different by being slimmer or more muscular and also to have enough breath and energy to succeed in our chosen task.

So if we go on a diet, pump iron and run 5 miles a day we will be fit! Won't we?

Well the answer to that is no! You would certainly make improvements within these areas that you are conditioning but you are still not fit!

Fitness is such a complex thing and books like '*Fit to Fight*' by Peter Consterdine and the '*Training videos*' by Kevin O'Hagan will certainly put you on the right path of increasing areas of your fitness; but in this book I want to give you a brief insight into fitness at its most basic and understandable level.

I believe that one of my writing qualities is to take a complex subject and translate that into easy, clear, understandable language that everybody can understand which you will already know this if you have read any of my other five books.

I can remember when learning to drive and looked for publications on the mechanics of a motor vehicle.

The books I found were so complex and non-reader friendly that I gave up struggling with them. I was then shown the Ladybird book of 'The Motor Car.' It all then fell into place and taught me that you can explain something in a technically brilliant fashion which only the chosen few will understand and absorb, or you can get back to entry level explanation of a subject and the majority will absorb and understand what it is that you are trying to say. So there lies my reason as to why I am going to explain fitness at the level that I am going to present to you in this book. Fitness is more complex than I am explaining here and needs to be tailored to suit different desired outcomes. For instance the fitness training of a Thai boxer will differ to that of a gymnast. My field of expertise is self-protection at street level, and it's with this in mind that I write this chapter.

In simplistic terms there are five areas that make up your fitness, which we call components. Let's take a look at each of them

The Five Components Are

1. Cardio-Respiratory.
2. Muscular Flexibility.
3. Motor Fitness skills/ability.
4. Muscular Strength.
5. Muscular endurance.

1. Cardio-Respiratory. (C/R)
The essence of 'life or death' fitness is the effective functioning of the Heart and Lungs. The C/R system is also the hardest to understand because it is the only component of fitness that is not outwardly visible.

The C/R system consists of 2 elements:-
1.Heart and blood vessels i.e. the Cardio-vascular system.
2.Lungs and airways.
The other components of fitness are important but not essential for the continuation of life.

In 1984, American fitness 'expert' Jim Fixx, who wrote the book entitled 'The Complete Book of Running', died whilst jogging. This led to a panic about the dangers of jogging. However the cause of death was discovered to be smoking, poor diet and a family history of heart disease. There is a difference between fitness and a healthy lifestyle!!

In a basic self-protection class like mine where the whole lesson on focussed on winning a fight before you even take a breath and little C/R exercise is taken, C/R fitness is not being addressed so I suggest to students that because it is the most important component of Fitness, they should seek other training outside of my class that will develop their C/R fitness. Here are some ideas;

Activities that promote C/R*

Jogging
Swimming
Cycling
Football Training
Boxing
Full Contact Karate/kickboxing
Rugby Training
Brisk Walking

*All need to be sustained for 20 minutes plus.

Activities that do not promote C/R

A non C/R orientated - self defence class
Golf
Darts
Snooker
Motor Racing
Table Tennis
Yoga
Slow walking to your car

Improving C/R Performance and Self-Protection

Examples could be :- **Running.** How far can you sprint? How many steps do you need to take over a measured distance if chased? This could relate to parking a car and being able to sprint back to it comfortably in an emergency if threatened with attack.

If a person cannot afford expensive equipment such as, a running machine etc. exercise such as skipping, shadow boxing, sustained bag-work or steps will help.

Aerobics and Anaerobics

Aerobics are exercises designed to increase the oxygen content of the blood over a sustained period of time.

Anaerobics, are exercise that use the oxygen already present in the blood i.e. short bursts as in a physical confrontation, which only lasts a few seconds will use the oxygenated blood currently within our body, without having to draw in more air, in order to re-oxygenate the used oxygenated blood cells. The anaerobic reserve of oxygenated blood will be used up rapidly within the first 10-12 seconds of an explosive encounter leaving an untrained person exhausted. You will then need to gasp for breath and take in more air, which then takes us into aerobic work. A short rest will restore some of the energy.

To use an analogy:- a car battery will only turn the engine over a few times before if starts to die. However it will regain some of its former energy if left for a minute or two. 'Clinching' in fights and boxing bouts is usually a sign of anaerobic exhaustion initially going into aerobic exhaustion, which should be recognised and taken advantage of.

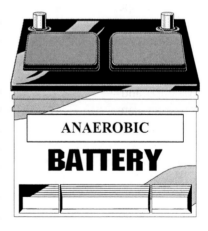

ANAEROBIC

BATTERY

30

Flexibility

This is the full range of movement of the joints from a starting point to a finishing point.

Flexibility deteriorates with age. E.g. many older people cannot store things on high shelves. So they store items of food on lower shelves, which are easier to reach within their range of flexibility.

Flexibility can be improved by Yoga or Tai Chi but, in a self-protection system; stretching and flexibility exercises should always relate to techniques in order to make sure that you are going to be able to perform your technique through its full cycle when needed.

Psycho-Motor Fitness

The three components of Psycho-Motor fitness are :-

1. Speed.   **2.** Balance.   **3.** Co-ordination.

This is explained in detail in my book '*What makes tough guys tough*' but to give you a brief example; Look at a Juggler, cyclist, or gymnast. These individuals clearly display what it looks like to have speed, balance and co-ordination working together in harmony. We must do the same with our self-protection moves to ensure they work together flowingly. Partner work and the use of training aids improve this component. This component is destroyed rapidly by alcohol consumption and some types of drugs.

Muscular Strength

This is basically where muscle groups overcome a maximum resistance. Many people only do this once a year when carrying heavy suitcases to the airport. Weight training will strengthen muscle groups.

In self-protection strength is not essential but is a real advantage in grappling. Strength can be improved by grappling training. My reason for stating that strength is not essential is because the

majority who are at risk of attack, that being female, children and the elderly, can still be taught to protect themselves without lifting weights or taking up wrestling. However they will never be contenders for the brutal 'Ultimate Challenge Fights.'

Muscular Endurance

This is the sub-maximum resistance that can be overcome over a period of time i.e. 60% of strength repetitively over a single period of time. An example of this would be to use a manual foot pump to put air into a tyre.

Muscular endurance can be increased by repetition so for Self-protection you would need to keep practising the same technique or combination repetitively.

The Big Question

So the big question here is, are you currently training in each one of the five components of fitness? If you can HONESTLY say yes; then you are addressing fitness within your training.

If you are training in some of the components of fitness, see if you can relate the training more to your self-protection preferences. The components that you are not actively training in do so, but again try to relate it to your self-protection system as closely as possible. For instance if you are lacking in aerobic fitness; this book will show you how to finish a fight in seconds before you even need to draw a breath. How to do it within your anaerobic capabilities.

You can then work on things such as your Aerobic fitness by doing short sprints to your car to simulate running away from an attacker, gradually parking the car further away over a period of time. This puts much more meaning into what you are doing rather than the boring old treadmill.

I used to do a 5-7 mile jog on my running machine each day until I realised that it was becoming a meaningless run unconnected to my desired outcome. I donated my machine to a local martial arts school who were training competition fighters and now do the car scenario where I am training my C/R but getting it as close as possible to my own self-protection needs. The running machine is now used by competition fighters who benefit more from this due to their intended outcome. It's horses for courses, as the saying goes!

Some Occupations and their Relationship to Fitness

Body Builders
This group train to improve outer appearance only; not for overall fitness. Neither are they training for muscular strength. They practice lots of muscular endurance work through repetition. They inevitably lose flexibility as their bulk increases if they do not work on their flexibility. Many also neglect C/R and Motor Fitness components because they are not needed for demonstration purposes.

Power Lifters
Train for muscular strength and muscular endurance more than appearance. No C/R component. Anaerobic strength needs to be developed i.e. short lived, explosive energy.

Doormen/Bouncers
(Untrained i.e. 90%)
Normally only have anaerobic ability and muscular strength. The first 10-12 seconds of an encounter with one

of these guys is normally decisive in the outcome. Someone with good level of C/R fitness could create a challenge for an untrained doorman if they avoid the initial encounter.

Street Thug/Attacker

Here you have your real life anaerobic guy with normally only this lone component of his components of fitness.

If your field of study is self-protection

Have a serious think about the fitness training that you currently promote and partake in yourself and decide if you are fit? Or fit for nothing!

The Alternative to Grappling

Technically there is no alternative to grappling. As soon as somebody takes a hold of you, be it standing or on the ground, you are in a potential grappling situation that you will have to break free from. Even a child could play wrestle you to the floor with the right trip, push, double leg grab, or rugby tackle. Even if you are standing, a child is quite capable of playfully holding on; forcing you to use some form of grappling technique at a mild level in order to gain release. So to be honest, there is no alternative to grappling apart from never coming into contact with another person.

Why then would I write a book subtitled *'The alternative to Grappling?'* Well my reason for doing so is to give you some preventative measures that you can take to make your stay within a grappling scenario as brief as two ships passing in the night. Or even better, avoid street grappling altogether.

Flavour of the month tells us that we should all be learning to grapple for our next street encounter. Well wake up folks! No matter how much you feel like crashing your elbows, knees, shoulders, head etc into the concrete today, it's the last place you want to be; so how about attempting to take a few steps back and see what we can do to avoid getting into a grappling scenario.

Guess what?

Shoes are designed to protect our feet from getting damaged and soiled on concrete, glass, metal, wood, dog shit (below), and that most attractive deposited ball of phlegm that some dirty bastard had just coughed up, along with many other hazardous and unpleasant things.

The rest of our body is not designed to come into contact with the city's pavements, which is why our shoes are designed with rubber or leather soles, rather than our clothes. Doesn't that tell you anything?

We are not designed to roll about on the floor. For this pastime we are given sandy beaches, beds, li-lo's, and the Red Sea. Why on earth would you want to go to ground for anything other than relaxing or lovemaking, unless you're a worm of course, but they don't have a choice, you do.

When I worked as a doorman and it kicked off, I never once said to myself

'I think I will take that guy to the floor to sort him out.' That, to me, would be like saying

'How can I fight this guy but first make the odds against me surviving much higher?' Maybe because I have had countless fights on the door and in the street, I see things differently? To me, when a kick-off situation occurs I get a message in my head saying,

'This guy is concealing an edged weapon that will cut, maim or kill me if he gets a hold of me' I then base the whole encounter around that one line. Doesn't this change the whole perspective of grappling in the street?

Ok! I'm no expert on knife fighting but having been stabbed twice, slashed viciously once and minor slashed a few times in the hundreds of violent encounters that I have had; I think that my one liner *'This guy is concealing……etc'* has saved my life.

(You can read about these in my book 'Thugs, Mugs and Violence')
Now, if I went into all the encounters that I have had with the frame of mind *'What arm bar should I use'* or *'Should I use a time hold or finishing hold on this guy'* I truly believe that I would be dead, blinded, or seriously maimed now.

Most of the encounters that I have had in nightclubs, pubs and the like were as a doorman. I cannot think of any other occupation that puts you in the dangerous role of having to possibly fight for your life every time you go to work.

Go and ask 100 doormen about fighting from the floor and see how many funny looks you get. You will not find any serious participant within the door supervision world that will suggest that you should fight from the floor. In fact most of them never fight from the floor, and never will, so what is going on here?

I'm telling you in one breath that the people that get in the most encounters of physical confrontation are doormen, then I am also telling you that I have been dragged to the floor many a time? It doesn't all add up does it?

Well the reason is that, most doormen fights are *'coconut shy fights.'* Just as in a fairground you get to line up your powerful well aimed strike with the objective of knocking the coconut from its shy, the doorman also mostly gets to line up the head/chin of the person that they want to strike. Hence, the fight is over before the recipient knows what's going on. This is coconut shy fighting and using this method it's easy to clock up dozens of successes without getting into grappling!

So don't doormen get into grappling fights?

You bet your life they do but it's not common except when they are ambushed, slip over or for some other reason they have ended up rolling about with somebody. I saw one doorman go to ground because he couldn't fight and was holding on for dear life waiting for help to arrive.

The sort of thing I did as a kid, holding on to stop myself getting a beating until a teacher came along to save me!
This brings me onto the next question, so where do grappling encounters happen then?

The answer to that is simple!

From the school playground right up to the street encounter. They happen in the real world of street fights.

I once wrote an article in the magazine 'Martial Arts Illustrated' entitled 'Grappling for Headless Chickens.'
Here is that article to give you another insight into the world of grappling.

Grappling for Headless Chickens

Grapple, Grapple, Grapple, It's all we hear these days in the martial arts. Martial artists are running around like headless chickens in a panic to learn the grappling arts but for most of them they are missing one vital point. For what reason do they want to learn to grapple? Is it for the street encounter? The ring? or the dojo? This seems to be the main question that skips by them in this panic search to add grappling skills to their database of techniques.

My area of expertise is the street, the street is my ring! So I will look at grappling from the street survival, point of view.

In my guise as a doorman I have been in 'rolling about on the floor' confrontations more times than I have been known to smile. I have ended up fighting from the floor for my personal survival for a variety of reasons ranging from slipping on a wet dancefloor, to being ambushed and dragged to the floor as you may have read about in my book 'Thugs, Mugs & Violence.' One thing that I can assure you in all honesty; is that fighting from the floor is the last place I ever wanted to be. However being as I am as good at grappling as I am at calorie control intake, I have had no alternative other than to just think 'Survive.' Survival instinct rapidly takes over and overrides any inferior grappling skills that I possess and was always well supported by my back-up system of a good set of teeth. Using my 'Biting fighting' that I have become known for, due to my book 'Dogs Don't Know Kung Fu', I have been able to deal with every groundfighting encounter that has come my way. As ugly as biting may seem, but it works!

Unfortunately though for us within the martial arts, we are encouraged to play fair when fighting and to use martial art techniques in a certain fashion. That's fine if you are good at your art and have confidence in it working for you when you get ambushed and dragged to the floor, but for me personally I find it much easier to sink my teeth into an attacker cutting hard and deep as required to gain release rather than to try and fight stylish by trying to get that brilliant arm bar or sleeper hold on.

So do I think that Sleeper holds, arm bars, pins, submission and finishing holds are of no use in the street grappling scenario? Not so, they are all great and necessary techniques to aid you in your survival **but** do not rely on them solely as the ultimate and only answer to dealing with a grappling situation.

Am I also appearing to deny the success of the grappling arts because I'm a Karate guy who has never been into a grappling art?

Wrong again, I began grappling in 1974 as a kid with the British Judo Association and coached my own son to gold medal standard, which he won in 1992. I also learnt Olympic Freestyle at the police training grounds in Wanstead near to where I live and have mixed and matched grappling techniques from all arts.

One of my closest advisors on grappling is my friend Kevin who came third in the British Olympic Freestyle Wrestling Championships, so I have my fair share of exposure to grappling. I will still say though, with my hand on my heart, that my personal grappling skills are pretty poor and have utmost respect for any grappling art. However I still do not promote its study as the ultimate range from which to fight from in the street. For me that range is punching along with other hand techniques.

You cannot ignore the fact that it is very likely that you will be taken to ground in a street encounter either by being punched down, dragged, slipping over, or ambushed **but** it is also very unlikely that you are going to be taken to the pavement by a grappling expert.

So if this is the case then, I can hear your thoughts saying '*If I'm a good grappler then I will beat the non grappler*' This may be the case technically but replace the words 'non grappler' with something more realistic like a '*panicking ruthless headbutting knife merchant*' and you will see things a little differently.

Now say the sentence '*If I'm a good grappler then I will beat the panicking ruthless headbutting knife merchant.*' It puts a much different perspective on things doesn't it?

There is more chance of you ending up on the floor with a panicking, headbutting, punching, weapon-welding attacker than something that you can classify simply as a non-grappler.

The grappling arts are great and have been the biggest 'wake up call' the U.K. martial arts have had since 'Full Contact' rocked our boats in the 70s. Geoff Thompson and Peter Consterdine are guilty of giving us the grappling 'wake up call' but don't let that take anything away from the dozens of other instructors of the grappling arts that live and breathe grappling. It's these guys that were studying and rigorously training in the grappling arts whilst people like myself, Geoff and Peter were marching up and down in white karate suits promoting Karate as being the be all and end all of the fighting arts. Credit must be given where credit is due.

One such guy that comes to mind is Dave Turton. Dave is no world champion, no publicity seeker, and like myself, no good looker, but when it comes to teaching the grappling arts, he's the man, although he will sleeper hold me for saying so. Get down to Rotherham to his full-time martial arts studio and get some good tuition in grappling. You can read what Dave has to say in my book 'What Makes Tough Guys Tough.' Kevin O'Hagan the author of 'I Thought You'd Be Bigger' is another guy to check out for floor work as is Darrin Richardson in Gosport. There are many more out there. If 'you' are one of these individuals, make yourself known and share your knowledge.

So, as you can see, I have bundles of respect for the grappling arts but having been stabbed twice in a groundfighting situation and dragged to the ground more times than I can remember, I still put the success of my survival down to 'biting fighting.'

Another thing to consider is how long we have known and practised a technique for?

Well, the method of using our teeth to bite and tear has been with us since the first day we possessed teeth and began to indulge in solid food. We were given teeth for the sole purpose of being able to tear and chew something to pieces. Even as toddlers most of us were told not to bite because it hurts.

From the first day of using our teeth consisting of approx. 30 edged weapons we have been training our biting and tearing skills to perfection. There is no other technique in your arsenal of weaponry that has had so much practice and been drilled as many times as your biting skills.

If you think a little more about how most animals have always defended themselves? Again it's all down to their ability to fight with their teeth. We buy dogs to protect our homes, but not because they know martial arts or grappling, dogs don't know kung fu! It's because of their biting ability. Nobody would buy a toothless dog for self-protection.

So where do you go from here? Do you chase about like a headless chicken panicking about which grappling art to learn? Do you forget the grappling arts in favour of 'biting fighting.?'

My advice to you is do both. Take on board 'biting fighting' as your instant release technique in order to survive and also learn the grappling arts, but focus on where it is that you want your grappling art to work. If it's in the street then use it as a support system, as and when you are proficient at it.

Don't lose your life trying to be 'Mr or Mrs Grapple'. If street grappling ever becomes the solution to eradicating rape then I will be the first to hold my hands up and put it in front of 'biting fighting' but until then my advice is to keep those teeth working but always bear in mind the risk of cross-contamination. For those of you that have no teeth and cannot bite! I do have another two alternatives to grappling in 'Dogs Don't Know Kung Fu' The choice is yours!

Some Types of Wrestling

Wrestling has become popular with martial artists due to grappling becoming flavour of the month. Most martial artists though, are training to be attacked by a particular style or method of grappling. We must never forget that street encounters are not bound by style or rules.

I want to introduce you to a few different types of wrestling so that you can decide for yourself if any aspects of these grappling related arts could benefit you in self-protection. Also it will give you an insight into what you can expect if you ever came across one of the players of these arts.

I am not going to list every form of wrestling because this is not the book for that, I just want to inform you of some of the more obscure formats of this art so you can have a think as to which pre-emptive strike you would use if faced with one of these exponents, and would you change it according to the type of wrestling or grappling that you are faced with?

Another point here is; If you think that the chance of you coming up against a grappler from one of the types of wrestling below, what makes you think that you are going to face the type of organised grappler that you are currently training towards.

Steer Wrestling also called BULLDOGGING, is a rodeo event in which a mounted cowboy on horseback chases a full-grown steer, dives from his horse on top of the animal, grasps its horns, digs his heels in the ground to bring the animal to a stop, and twists it to the ground flat on its side with all four legs and head in the same direction and the cowboy still in contact. Now what if the mounted cowboy transferred his rodeo skills into a barroom brawl with you?

Catch-as-Catch-Can Wrestling is a basic wrestling style in which nearly all holds and tactics are permitted in both upright and ground wrestling. Rules usually forbid only actions that may injure an opponent, such as strangling, kicking, gouging, and hitting with a closed fist.

The object is to force the opponent into a position in which both shoulders touch the ground at the same time. Formerly known as the Lancashire style in England, catch-as-catch-can became the most popular form of wrestling in Great Britain and the United States and, with slight modifications, was introduced into Olympic and International competition as freestyle wrestling.

The interesting thing here about the art is the things that they have actually banned because they are considered dangerous. An obvious choice here would be to use the strangling, kicking, gouging, and hitting with a closed fist along with everything else you know in order to fight back.

Greco-Roman Wrestling is style of wrestling practised in Olympic and International amateur competition. In Greco-Roman wrestling the legs may not be used in any way to obtain a fall, and no holds may be taken below the waist. Other rules and procedures for Greco-Roman wrestling are the same as those for freestyle wrestling.

Greco-Roman wrestling originated in France in the early 19th century, in imitation of classical Greek and Roman representations of the sport. It became favoured in Scandinavian countries and Swedish and Finnish wrestlers won many Olympic titles from 1912 to 1948, after which the Soviet Union and other countries came to the fore.

Cornish Wrestling is a style of wrestling developed, and still practised, in south-western England. It is also known as the Cornwall and Devon, or West Country style. Cornish wrestlers wear stout, loose canvas jackets; rules allow wrestlers to take hold anywhere above the waist or by any part of the jacket, although any manipulation of the jacket collar to strangle an opponent is forbidden. A fall is gained when hips and a shoulder or both shoulders and a hip touch the ground simultaneously but wrestling on the ground is forbidden. Tripping and other uses of the legs are very important, and in Devon, wrestlers formerly wore heavy-soled shoes, with which it was legitimate to kick an adversary's shins.

Cumberland Wrestling is a form of wrestling developed in northern England and southern Scotland, also called the North Country style. The wrestlers stand chest-to-chest, each grasping the other with locked hands around the body, each opponent's chin on the other's right shoulder. The right arm is placed below and the left above the adversary's. When the hold has been firmly taken, an umpire gives the word to start and the bout proceeds until one man touches the ground with any part of his person except his feet or fails to retain his hold. In either case he loses. If both fall together, the one who is underneath or first touches the ground loses. If both fall simultaneously side-by-side (a dogfall), the bout begins anew. The manoeuvres used to throw an adversary are called chips. There is but a single foul-direct kicking. British championships in this style are held annually.

Schwingen is a form of wrestling native to Switzerland and the Tirolese valleys. Wrestlers wear '*Schwinghosen*' (wrestling breeches) with strong belts on which holds are taken. Lifting and tripping are common, and the first man down loses the bout. *Schwingen* tournaments were organised as early as 1805

Sambo is also described as Russian: 'self-defence without weapons.' It is a form of wrestling developed in the Soviet Union but also practised in Japan and Bulgaria. In 1964 it was recognised by the International Federation of Amateur Wrestling. It is similar to both judo and freestyle. Strangling, kicking and scratching are among the few tactics forbidden.

Pancratium is an ancient Greek sports event that combined boxing and wrestling, where savage hitting, kicking, twisting of limbs, strangling, and struggling on the ground were allowed. However biting and gouging were not allowed. A contest ended when one of the fighters acknowledged defeat.

Sumo Wrestling is a style of Japanese wrestling in which weight, size, and strength are of the greatest importance, though speed and suddenness of attack are also useful. The object is to topple and propel the opponent out of a ring or to force him to touch the ground with any part of his body other than the soles of his feet. The ring covers an area of about 15 feet. The wrestlers wear only loincloths and grip each other by the belt.

Add to all this the better known arts of Judo and Olympic Freestyle Wrestling along with the many offshoot and other Grappling related arts, you realise that wrestling is a very large practised art. However your chances of coming up against a wrestler, Brazillian Ju-Jitsu guy or any form of grappler other that the street fighter is very remote. One thing to also bear in mind as well is that all these arts are governed by rules. Even the brutal 'Ultimate Fighting Championships' are bound by rules.

Rules – Rules – Rules!

Forget about them if you want to win a fight and most important of all; win that fight with your pre-emptive strike!

Peter Consterdine from the British Combat Association says

'Over the past few years, particularly with the advent of the UFC, grappling has enjoyed a revival. Don't think though that being good at grappling will make you good in the street. If going to ground is your first option then you are going to have big problems. Grappling skills should be sufficient enough to raise confidence if you do go to the ground, but not enough that you would want to stay there. There should be enough skill to overcome the panic and freeze that grips people who have not come from a grappling background. Far better that you become excellent at vertical grappling - so that you can put your opponent to the floor, without going yourself.'

Check out the video by Peter Consterdine and Geoff Thompson Pavement arena part 3 – Grappling – the last resort.

Peter also states in his book *'Streetwise'*

'Your overriding single goal when you are taken to the ground is to recover your feet ASAP. However you achieve this is OK, but get back up you must.'

In the book *'Real Grappling'* by Geoff Thompson, Geoff says:

'Grappling techniques should be employed as a last resort, to back up a failed punch (your own punch) or to combat a 'blind side' grab.'

Geoff has become very well known for his promotion of the grappling arts but still clearly states in his book *'Dead or alive'* that
'To throw yourself into a grappling situation to fight your attacker is tantamount to throwing yourself at his mercy.'

Forget the Rules and Use Your Tools

Here are a few examples of people that didn't want to play by anybody else's rules and decided that the pre-emptive strike was the best option for their survival!

In 1807 the entire Danish fleet was taken after England's pre-emptive naval actions. This brought to an end Denmark-Norway's attempt to remain neutral in the struggle between France and England and their respective allies early in the 19th century.

The Israeli Cabinet decided on a pre-emptive strike when Egyptian and Iraqi troops arrived in Jordan, giving every sign of an imminent pan-Arab attack. The Israeli air force destroyed Nasser's planes on the ground, and in six days of fighting (June 5-10 1967) The Israeli air force caught the Egyptian air force on the ground, largely destroying the Arab world's most effective military force. In Sinai in the following days the Israeli army smashed the Egyptian troops. An estimated 10,000 Egyptians died.

The Japanese attack at Pearl Harbour was a pre-emptive strike to gain command of the western Pacific. Simultaneously, Japanese forces attacked the Philippines, Malaya, and the Dutch East Indies. More than 180 aircraft were destroyed. U.S. military casualties totalled more than 3,400, including more than 2,300 killed. The Japanese lost less than 100 men

----

Lets now relate the term Pre-emptive strike to street 'self-protection'
(This is a true story)
Gisela Braun realised that she had just hitched a lift from the 'Devil's Moor Murderer' and was about to become his 13th victim. One of his previous victims was strangled & stabbed 57 times. Gisela was not skilled in the Martial Arts or any other type of self-defence system, but she knew clearly that her life was at stake.

She decided to stall for time, knowing every second could have been her last. In reply to being told to strip, she said to the attacker,

'I don't mind doing it with you, but I'm a bit worked up. Let me smoke a cigarette first. It always gets me in the mood.'

The Devils Moor murderer thought that she was not aware of whom he was or what he was about to do to her, so he did not hesitate to light up her cigarette. Gisela took a long drag on the cigarette until the end glowed red, then with a quick movement, pressed it into the man's left eye.

He screamed in pain as he clutched his face, while she tripped the door handle, sprang out of the car and ran off into the dark. As he switched on his lights to try to find her, she read his lighted numberplate and scratched the registration into the earth.

The result was she survived and he was traced the next day and was subsequently sentenced to confinement for the remainder of his life, in an institution for the criminally insane.

The successful outcome was due to a cigarette being used as a weapon in a pre-emptive strike to prevent the attack. Just think about it!

This extract was taken from my book *'Dogs Don't Know Kung Fu – the guide to female self protection.'*

Another Way of Looking at it!

Have you heard of Preventive medicine?

The reason it is used in 'well' people is to reduce or eliminate the risks associated with disease. Prevention is a form of pre-emptive strike that hopes to avert disease before it develops.

An example of this would be to vaccinate children against diseases like Measles, Mumps and Rubella by pre-emptively giving the MMR injection.

In 1796 Surgeon Edward Jenner, discoverer of vaccination for smallpox, realised that cowpox not only protected against smallpox but also could be transmitted from one person to another as a pre-emptive strike and form of protection against the cowpox attack on the body.

Fear and the Pre-emptive Strike

Fear is a phobia or a mixture of phobias. Fear is explained in detail and in a much more comprehensive way than I can cover here in the book, *'Fear-The Friend of Exceptional People'* by Geoff Thompson, which is one of my favourite books of all time.
I will do my best here to talk about fear in relation to this book.

Most people suffer from an extreme, irrational fear of a specific object or situation. It's a phobia and type of anxiety disorder which is the main symptom experienced by the sufferer.
Phobias are thought to be learned emotional responses, which are all part of our 'affective learning', which you can read more about in my book *'What Makes Tough Guys Tough.'*
Fear mostly happens when a prior-threatening situation is remembered, even subconsciously, when a similar situation occurs at another time in our life, even if the original reason for our fear is long forgotten.
In my book *'Thugs, Mugs and Violence'* I talk about when I was a non-swimmer dragged under water. Later in life I could be in a situation of violence that I find easy to handle, but change the scenario and environment to fighting on a boat and falling overboard; then the situation changes! My fear for drowning wipes out any self-protection skills that I have.
My fear of water is based on a childhood experience of almost drowning. The person accordingly tries to avoid that situation in the future, a response that, while reducing anxiety in the short term, reinforces the person's association of the situation with the onset of anxiety. In theory, if I was gradually exposed to the anxiety-provoking situation of the swimming pool in a controlled manner, I should eventually cease to feel anxiety but I haven't pursued this challenge.
I have however pursued this challenge within other areas of my life that are also important; that being self-protection. As a child I was bullied, scared of fighting, afraid of feeling physical pain and so on. Basically, I was a wimp – a victim – a target.

As I grew older and had the odd two to three hundred fights (No exaggeration) I eventually became desensitised to it and 20 years on I was working as a doorman in some of the roughest clubs in London & Soho.

To digress a bit.

The word 'phobia' which is from the Greek word for the 'object feared' is attached to most titles used to describe a type of fear

Among the more common examples are Nyctophobia, fear of the dark; Xenophobia, fear of strangers; Claustrophobia, fear of closed places; Ochlophobia, fear of crowds.

Add all these phobias to a confrontation and your fear to launch a pre-emptive strike and you have a minefield of problems.

For many years I 'feared' launching a pre-emptive strike because of the dangers that were attached to it.

I feared that my pre-emptive strike would not work, leaving my attacker to continue with his attack.

I feared the pre-emptive strike would enrage the attacker even more resulting in an even worse physical attack on myself.

I feared the success of my pre-emptive strike because I envisaged the dangers of a comeback from my attacker to seek revenge.

I found every possible way to 'fear' launching a pre-emptive strike that I could.

I won't go into detail of how I overcome this fear, because it's extensively covered in my book 'Thugs, Mugs and Violence.' What I will tell you here is that you are never going to throw your pre-emptive unless you are commanded to, just as a sprinter on the starting block waiting for the gun to fire.

You probably already have a physical technique that you are capable of launching and are comfortable with from your own chosen fighting system. You know that you can launch this strike with speed and power, so what is stopping you from doing so?

Basically, you are waiting to be given permission! The command to go, the word, indication or something similar, which will trigger off the launch of your pre-emptive weapon.

My method is kind of like following the reverse order of a traffic light.

Red = Stop

For me this represents, Red = **Danger** and **Stop**; meaning Stop daydreaming and switch on.

Amber = Get ready

Amber for me represents get ready to launch my attack and make sure there is an opening for it to land.

Green = Go

Green for me is time to go, or rather, time for my pre-emptive strike to go!

I personally use a word that has always found its way to my vocal cords when I am at an explosive enraged state of mind. That word is 'C**t., as in CU Next Tuesday!

I either say it in my head to myself if I'm in company of the police, CCTV, or my mother. Other than that I scream it out as viciously as I can to get the attention of the person I'm about to hit by engaging his brain.

When the green light switches on in my head, my pre-emptive strike will have left its ready position and will have struck the target within my scream of "You C**t!."

As a young lad I used a different method because most of my serious fights were in nightclubs and pubs where the verbal scream could not be heard above the live band or DJ. It was a pretty unique system that still works to this day and can be found in my book *'Thugs, Mugs and Violence'*

I am not suggesting that you adopt my traffic light system. Find one that suits you better, if not, try mine. Also don't confuse this with the survival awareness, colour code system, taught by Peter Consterdine & Geoff Thompson. That's something completely different…

The philosopher Aristotle observed that,

'Anger is caused by undeserved slight, fear by the perception of danger, but no one fears when angry'

Maybe this could explain why my own personal Pre-emptive strikes work wonderfully well when I explode with my *"You c**t!"* phrase when my green light tells me to 'go!'

For that fraction of a second any fear that I have will be wiped out by my anger and enraged emotions. All I know is that it works for me..

Have a think about the phrase that you use when you get angry with your children, partner, boss, work colleagues etc. Then think about how close you have been to wanting to combine that with physical violence. Combine the two and add to this your pre-emptive strike and you will be capable of defeating your next attacker.

For those of you that abuse this ability to harm your partner, children, the elderly or animals. Stop now! Its wrong - you are no better than the rest of the scum out there that hurt, maim and kill innocent people. Don't think that just because you are doing it to someone that you know, its ok – it does not make it any less an evil cowardly bullying act.

If you are a bully or a victim of this type of situation, read my book *'Dogs Don't Know Kung Fu'* to understand how violence affects people, and how you can deal with it.

The Pre-emptive Psyche

Sometimes instead of a pre-emptive strike – you can use a pre-emptive psyche. We all have the ability to do it but for some of us it comes more natural.

Jamie with Peter Consterdine

Parents are always doing it to children as a form of warning to say 'If you carry on doing that – I will belt you.'

Many of us, as adults, can send the same 'I will belt you' message to another adult by looking, staring and psyching them out as our pre-emptive strike.

Or as I prefer to call it a 'Pre-emptive psyche'

As a doorman I have used the Pre-emptive Psyche probably every single night that I worked. It was definitely used 99% more times than my pre-emptive strike to deal with trouble customers. The same goes for the street encounters that I have had, the Pre-emptive psyche has saved my bacon many a time. The only time I can think that it was not too successful was in the school playground. I try now to stick to fighting adults of my own age and stay away from playground fights (Joking).

The Physical Side

We can talk all day and philosophise about what may and may not happen in a confrontation, but one thing that can be guaranteed for sure is that you are going to have to hurt some people in order to stop them hurting you.

So as I said earlier in the book, you are going to have to strike out pre-emptively, with speed, power and aggression.

Please wherever possible, use the techniques that you have drilled over time, from your own system of training that you feel comfortable with. There is no point in doing a new technique just because you see it work for me, Geoff Thompson, Peter Consterdine, Dave Turton, Kevin O'Hagan, Count Duckula or Hong Kong Fooey. Do what works for you!

If you like something that you have seen work for one of us then spend time practising it until you are confident that it will flow comfortably and work for you. Until then stick to what you know even if it's as obscure as 'The Kangaroo double heel kick' or a 'Squirrel nut cracking strike.'

I personally believe that I could take 'almost' any strike from any system of training and make it work for me. Its taken me 24 years to gain this ability so don't be put of if you cannot make someone else's technique work for you. Time and practice will solve that, if it's a technique that is personally suitable for your bodies' capabilities within the realms of reality.

It's not 'what you use' as a body weapon that decides the final outcome, the more important factor is 'How you use' your body weapon on your opponent that will make a difference to the result.

I.e. A full force fingertip strike to the beer gut will probably result in 'Beer belly' beating your brains in, but throw the same strike deep into his eye sockets, tickling his brain and I don't think he will be wanting to continue with his intended attack.

So as you can see, **how you use** something is more important than **what you choose** to use.

What Weapon to Choose

If you don't study a fighting system, the choice should be relatively easy. You will probably be able to count your options on one hand. You are very lucky!

For the likes of me who have studied every form of fighting that you can gain access to, it can be a real nightmare.

Which of our 1,001 techniques will we choose for our pre-emptive strike?

Being spoilt for choice is actually a hindrance at times.

I compare this to the difference between men and women going shopping. Men have only one shopping technique! They go out and buy the first thing that does the job and the whole ordeal is over in the shortest possible time.. Women however! Well that's a different ball game altogether! They have to go through every choice and option available to them, to get an end result.

We martial artists apply the female shopping concept to our choice of martial arts body weapons and techniques and wonder why we get our lights punched out, from time to time!

Wake up folks! And get rid of the long thoughtful martial arts method of choosing a weapon for your pre-emptive strike. Fit all your weapons of choice onto one hand. I.e. Fingertip jab, palm slap, head butt, pelvic kick, right cross.

Once you have narrowed it down you will be in a much better position than searching through you mental database of weaponry to find the strike of the day. It doesn't have to be five techniques, it can be three, but whatever number you choose they must all work for you and must be realistically be capable of stopping the attacker. Also most important of all, use techniques from your own system of training that you have drilled time and time again that you know that **you** can make work.

I personally label myself as being 'Style-less' meaning that I do not belong to or promote any particular style of training. I am a self-protection instructor with only one life and will use absolutely anything within my means, to protect myself if attacked.

If I try to fight according to the rules, regulations, or acceptability of any given system of training, I may lose my only life. I cannot afford to make that mistake just to promote a particular system of training or to not offend an instructor of any art that I have studied. Nobody has the right to tell me how to protect my own life by denouncing a technique or method of protecting my life that works for me.

You have a think about this - very seriously. How much is your life worth to you? Would you rather lose your life than offend your system of training because it would be frowned upon if you used a life saving technique that does not fit in with your syllabus? Please get a life – and – save a life…. Yours!

Please don't misunderstand the message I am trying to portray to you. I am not knocking your system of training. If anything, I strongly advise you to use your own system because you will be better at it than at something that you don't know.

What I am saying is 'If something works for you – even if it is frowned upon within you system of training – please use it because that may be the one thing that saves your life.'

I cannot think of a better place to use the quote 'Use it or lose it!' 'It' meaning your life!

To help you go through your arsenal of available weapons in order to narrow your choice I have developed a 'Style-less' method of storing my pre-emptive choices of attacking weapons. If you want to research this further I suggest you check out my forthcoming book on 'How to develop your own personal fighting system.'

The following part of the book goes into the storage and retrieval of pre-emptive strikes using my 'head to toe' concept.

I begin at the highest point of my body and think of a strike that I could launch effectively against an opponent. My choice is to use my forehead to strike the aggressor. This we all know as the 'headbutt' or 'sticking the nut in.' You are now in the position of saying *'Yeah, I like that, I will use that as one of my strikes'* or *'My system of training doesn't endorse or allow headbutting.'*

You could even make the choice of *'That's fine, but my choice would be to start at the Crown and charge in like a bull.'*

Can you see what I'm getting at? Start at the top of your body and build your body weapons around that.

As you work your way down the body you will come across many conflicts and things that may clash with your style of training, plus you will introduced to the laws of reality, as to what would reasonably and practically work for you.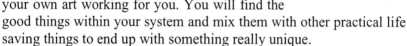

I promise you that if you use my system of storing pre-emptive strikes that work for you, you will become much more confident about your own art working for you. You will find the good things within your system and mix them with other practical life saving things to end up with something really unique.

Some of you will go from the headbutt then onto the elbow strike as your next capable pre-emptive strike. What about the 30 edged weapons that you have in your mouth that you can bite with? Ok, so you now include the pre-emptive bite so what's next, the elbow strike? Maybe, but what about you smokers out there, do your realise how painful the impact of 'Nicotine Saliva' is if you spit into someone's eyes! It burns-big time... It is still a valid and useful pre-emptive strike and I bet you something, even if you don't include it – you will always remember it.

My system of storing and retrieving your bodies weapons is unique to my own 'New Breed self protection system' but I teach it all over the world and it is always well received, so please give it a try. So! now we have got the 'Crown charging bull' technique out the way, along with the 'headbutt, biting and Nicotine spitting' can we now get on to the Elbow strike?

Sorry, not yet!

What about my speciality 'The  shoulder butt.' A brilliant technique that I have used generously at close range countless times. Even though this strike requires both hands to pull the persons Jaw & face into direct line with your shoulder tip at devastating speed, we do not go onto hand strikes now.

Although the hands could also deliver a ferocious double slap as it pulls the head down, it is the shoulder butt that we are storing here for later retrieval.

Now we can go onto the elbow strikes and so on until we get down to the toes. Head to feet is a more correct description but 'head to toe' rolls off the tongue much easier.

You should have the basic idea now as to how I am suggesting that you store your pre-emptive strikes. If you like this idea and want to learn more about it then I suggest that you (2nd book plug coming) get my book on 'How to develop your own personal fighting system.'

Remember that when you are storing your pre-emptive strikes, you must include all the things from your own system of training that work for you. Using my method of storage and retrieval working from head to toe you can insert pre-emptive strikes wherever you want regardless of style or system of training.

If you end up with 20 to 50+ different pre-emptive strikes that's fine. You have learnt a good way or storing and remembering them but don't forget about your final intended outcome, which is, for you to be able to narrow them down to a handful of 'Powerful, lethal strikes' so that one of them will stop the aggressor from proceeding with their intention to hurt you.

I will move on now to show you some techniques from my

'Head to toe–pre-emptive strike–storage and retrieval system©'

Sounds like something from a DIY store, doesn't it!

Yes folks! That is a copyright symbol above, that's how successful my method has become.

Don't let this affect your personal safety on the streets though; the copyright is enforceable to protect me from the 'entrepreneurial business sharks.'

My method is there to protect **you** from the 'Street sharks' so please use it. I won't sue you for using my system to save your life, honest! Tell me about your success stories, you never know, you may end up in my next book!

The Art of Prediction

Pre-emptive strikes rely heavily on prediction of what you think the likely outcome of a confrontation is going to be. The same can also be partly said for avoidance of grappling situations.

How often has it been said *'The attacker just came out from nowhere - without any warning – I didn't have a chance!'* or *'I was caught by complete surprise!.'*

These are very common quotes used after an ambush or surprise attack. The sad thing about this is, that many of these attacks 'were' seen in the form of warning signals by the victim at some stage before the attack took place in some shape or form.

The victim 'did' have some prior knowledge of the attack but refused to recognise it as such. In most situations pre-attack indicators were present before the attack took place but the victim discounted them as being unimportant. Attacks don't just happen, they are planned, whether it be a few minutes before the attack or a few weeks it was still planned at some stage before the attack happened.

Think about some of the high profile attacks such as Lennon, Kennedy, and Regan along with some of the lesser-known attacks like Smith, Jones and Bloggs. They all have something in common. 'They were all planned.'

So to aid you in your survival within everyday life, and to assist you in avoiding grappling, plus help you launch your pre-emptive strike, you must learn to understand a little more about the art of prediction in order to see a planned attack building up.

In my previous guise of a door supervisor and personal security personnel I would begin my art of prediction with 'visual scanning.' I would use my eyes like a submarine periscope to scan the full 360 degrees to search for anything that gives me a hunch, gut feeling, intuition or whatever you want to call it, something that does not fit into the surrounding setting as it should do.

The worst thing that could possibly happen if I was being over anxious is that I have triggered off a false alarm within myself.

The best thing that can happen is that I save my own, or somebody else's life. Now that can't be a bad thing can it?

To ensure that I do not get a 'cry wolf' situation every time it is a false alarm, and to avoid wrongly launching a pre-emptive strike, I would only share my information with others when I have comfortably predicted that a situation is going to occur, something being planned that is going to cause harm or an injustice to someone.

Visual scanning gives you the opportunity to spot an irregularity and question its existence before its too late. It allows you to use the art of prediction, to predict what you think the possible outcome may be, acting on the information that your senses have given you. Notice here that I say senses and not just eyes. Although what you initially see is very important, you must also take into account *'what you feel.'*

It could be a chemical reaction, a smell, or a sound etc that sends the message to your brain saying *'Something is not right here – I don't know what it is, but I just feel uncomfortable about this, get ready to launch a pre-emptive strike'*, some people call it intuition, a sixth sense or common sense.

For many of us though, even when we get that signal that something is not right, we proceed to ignore the warning and want to kick ourselves after a situation has gone wrong.

Here are some words that you may recognise.

'I just knew that I shouldn't have opened my door to him, I don't know why I did it?'

Or *'Something told me to not to walk home alone, yet I still did it. If only I would have listened to myself!'*

Comments like these are very common but are heard more outside of the self-protection environment because we do not get onto confrontations everyday, however the possibility of confrontation 'exists' every day.

How many car drivers have enraged you enough to induce anger, the passing thought of wanting to use violence and possibly even the desire to kill? It happens doesn't it?

So if this is the case, how many other people feel this way about you and the way that you drive?

All it takes is one person to be at the end of their tether and flip and you will have a situation that could result in you bruised, battered or dead. Have you seen the Michael Douglas film 'Fallen Down?.' The film is obviously an 'over the top' reaction by the character but never the less, the essence of the message is still there, that a build up of incidents on a bad day can turn someone into a walking time bomb..

You can take any situation at all and play the prediction game, guess what the possible outcome could be.

Nostradamus would predict future events and catastrophes, fortune-tellers predict your future, Astrologers predict how they think the stars are going to affect you, Gamblers predict the outcome of many things, Weather forecasters predict the weather, and so on.

Basically, everybody uses the art of prediction so why not use it as an aid to self-protection so that you can avoid even having to use a pre-emptive strike.

Lets look at a mock scenario to see where the art of prediction takes us.

I am walking my dog in the park where another dog owner is also walking his dog. My dog runs over to the other dog and playfully jumps on him, teases him and wants a little game. I call my dog back because I see that the other dog does not want to play. My dog returns to me but suddenly decides to go back for another attempt at playing with the dog. He barges into him then jumps all over him again. The dog's owner then aggressively calls out to me

'get your dog away from my dog otherwise, I will kick him if he does it again.'

Let's now play the prediction game! What are the possible outcomes?

I ignore the guy and let my dog carry on. My dog gets kicked and I go over to the guy and a fight evolves which also involves two dogs protecting their owners.

Either of us could become seriously hurt or at the extreme, killed.

I could go over to the guy and apologise for my dog's persistence. He sees my apology as a sign of weakness and proceeds to redirect his threat of violence towards me, again resulting in a physical confrontation.

I take exception to his threat towards my dog and make my way over to his dog and give the dog a beating.

I discipline my own dog by physically punishing him to pre-empt the other dog's owner kicking my dog.

I let the dogs fight.

I take a hold of my dog, ignore the guy's comments and walk in the opposite direction to avoid the situation getting uglier.

The guy comes over to me and begins a fight resulting in one or both of us leaving the park in a police car or ambulance.

Which of these options would you choose based on the possible predicted outcome, bearing in mind your own self-protection?

I personally, would like to have apologised to the guy because I realise that as a dog owner, I was being irresponsible by letting my dog run wild. For all I know the other dog could have been carrying pups, recovering from an operation, could be ill, or even a vicious animal trained to attack.

However as much as I would like to have apologised my 'gut feeling' told me that this situation could have quite easy, escalated into violence had I approached him. He had not directly threatened me, he did not kick my dog, rather he made an idle threat, also he did not offer a challenge directly to me but I was not happy with his mannerism or body language and 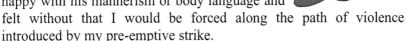 felt without that I would be forced along the path of violence introduced by my pre-emptive strike.

I decided to take hold of my dog and walk in the opposite direction, ignoring his comment. Although I would like to have apologised because I knew that I was in the wrong, my prediction of what could, and was likely to happen, stopped me.

Male bravado wanted me to punch his lights out but again the art of prediction and common sense wisely steered me away from this option, which I add would have been the wrong choice. I had been irresponsible as a dog owner and was at fault.

Now consider how the other guy must have felt. He made an idle threat, received no apology and still had his dog jumped on. I'm sure he went home with a sense of unhappiness, frustration and anger, knowing that he had neither carried out his idle threat nor forced an apology out of me. He also had the option to come over and further release his anger but rather, he took it home with him and probably unleashed it on some undeserving sole. I also may have been an undeserving sole from an encounter that had aggrieved him earlier on, before our paths crossed. As you may now have gathered, the dog scenario was a true case study rather than a mock scenario.

I used here a simple prediction process that would give me the most likely outcome of coming out of the situation unruffled, un-grappled and avoided my using a pre-emptive strike.. I try my hardest to apply this to every other situation and scenario in daily life when I receive that warning signal that something could escalate towards danger or a violent outcome.

However I'm far from perfect and do sometimes get it wrong and find I'm having to deal with things like a beer glass travelling at 30mph towards my face, or alternatively, have acted on my gut feeling, rather than thinking about the possible outcomes, putting someone to rest for a while with my pre-emptive strike.

But if you 'honestly' want to avoid physical violence and confrontation, you will have to act on the advice I have given, rather that using some of the violent counter methods that I have detailed in my books.

Some people I know would consider the prediction process as a cowardly method of dealing with possible confrontations, because you are always looking for the option that is going to steer you from harm, even if it does hurt your pride a little.

I say that you should let someone hurt your pride rather than let them hurt your body. It is a much harder thing to do, but with practice you will find it easier as you go along. Think about some of the situations that you have been in, and take the whole scenario backwards, a step at a time, to the very earliest point that you think that you could have predicted the outcome, and more importantly, have changed the outcome.

If you cannot think of one, try some of these: road rage, queue jumping, waiting to use a public telephone, drunks, noisy people at the pictures, and so on, as a starting point.

Spending half my life a bouncer/door supervisor, forced me into using the art of prediction in order to aid my own personal survival. I hope that you can now take on board this advice and have a future free from physical confrontation. However, if you are ever in doubt, remember that you only have that one life to protect, so you cannot leave anything to chance.

The Grey Area

Where does the balance lay between using a pre-emptive strike to protect ourselves, and actually becoming the attacker?

As I mentioned earlier, some people could freely abuse the whole pre-emptive strike thing if they were aware of it, especially those in the front line, like door supervisors.

In theory, as a door supervisor, I could strike out at anybody I wanted to, claiming that I feared for my safety. Technically and legally I could possibly get away with this for quite some time. However this would also technically and legally be wrong, if I was disguising and distorting the truth. Like, hitting people that did not make me fear for my safety, just because I enjoyed hitting people. They call that bullying where I come from.

If I only ever pre-emptively hit those that I 'truly' believed were going to harm me, I would be within my full rights to defend myself. Anything other than that would not justify my physical response, so this really does away with the grey area, doesn't it.

Well how about if you are not a doorman, and just the average guy/girl on the street, does this change anything?

The answer is no. Reason being that the legality of the pre-emptive strike is no different for the guy on the street than it is for a door supervisor. Self-defence is self-defence, no matter who you are. Door supervisors have no extra rights.

What about then, striking out at someone that is not attacking you; is not coming towards you, and is not making you fear for your safety. Are there circumstances that would cause or allow you to strike out without having being threatened with attack yourself? Of course there is!

Would you walk by and ignore an old lady being battered by a couple of youths?

Would you react if you came out of your house to see a stranger trying to pull your child by the hair, into their car?

Would you stop someone that you saw, pouring petrol over a live kitten, in order to set it on fire?

For these very same reasons and many others like them, people have brought it upon themselves to strike out the first blow, without initially being at risk of harm themselves or fearing for their safety.

In the eyes of the law, anybody would be justified in intervening in ugly situations like these where another person or animal is being harmed, or put into fear for their own safety. Nobody could dispute that, but what I am asking you now is to have a think as to, if you could legally perform a pre-emptive strike in any of the above scenarios, because you, feared for your 'own' safety. And if not, how could you 'abuse' the concept of the pre-emptive strike to lay claim that you 'did' fear for your own safety, which would justify your actions.

This little exercise should show whether or not, you have absorbed the whole pre-emptive strike thing!

Lets use some pictures to
Help with the message

Where possible, we have tried to avoid stylised body positioning and techniques, so as to cater for the untrained reader and also to encourage trained fighters
to use their own way.

Many techniques, especially Elbows, do not translate too well from reality to photograph. To the inexperienced eye this could come across as the different techniques looking the same. I do apologise for any confusion that this may cause and suggest that you seek out professional tuition to learn the individual psychomotor skills, if you cannot see the difference within each technique.

Forward Headbutt
Jaw-Face - Chest

Everybody knows about the headbutt, but here are a few other ways to consider throwing out this strike.
For example with hands in pocket.
Or from behind a newspaper, which screens the visual warning that it is on its way, plus it helps avoid cross contamination from blood etc if you produce an open wound.

Straight into the centreline of the chestplate which is ideal if there is a difference in height.

If you are going to perform this strike to the head, make sure it's below the eyeline for it to be most effective.

Down Headbutt to Collar Bone

The collarbone is very easily broken, and will leave the injured person unable to continue with an attack on you.

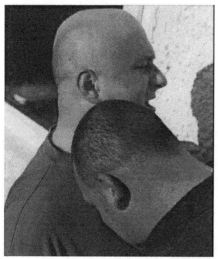

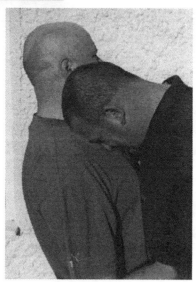

Rear Headbutt

This rear strike is best served to the nose, which is very effective due to the numerous nerves it contains.

Although not a technique that you would normally consider outside of a rear bear hug, I have used it once effectively in a nightclub whilst working as a doorman, when a close whisper from behind kindly offered to beat my brains in.

I also have a friend who used the rear headbutt effectively to deal with a pickpocket as they were travelling down the underground escalator.

Bite

Not the type of pre-emptive strike that immediately comes to mind, however in a situation where you are pinned to a wall, or restricted by space or in a car or phone box, it could come as a real shock to the recipient.

Shoulder-butt

Probably my most favourite close range technique. One that I have used generously.

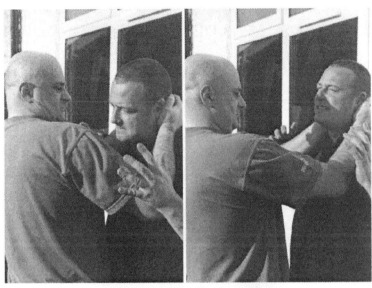

Forward Elbow Jab

Best used to chest-plate whilst driving full bodyweight directly following elbow jab.

Throw elbow in and out in the same manner as you would a boxing jab.

Forward Round Hook Elbow

Very powerful if you have the angle right, Best areas of impact are the centreline of chest plate and side of the head, with elbow tip.

Forward Reverse Hook Elbow

The pulling motion of this elbow strike can be devastating, especially to the side of neck and temple.

Rising Elbow

A good strike if you are restricted from moving or you are within comfortable range of the 'under chin' area.

Side Elbow

Very effective at close range with minimum risk of damage to yourself. Most powerful if you are able to push beyond the point of impact, or thrust in and out quickly.

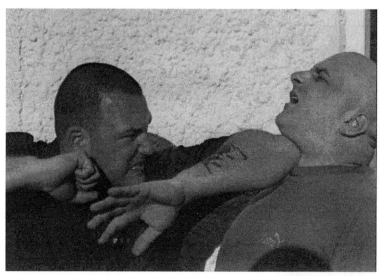

Rear Elbow

A classic strike universal too most striking training systems. Many people perform this strike to the stomach area but for a more devastating strike use the tip of the elbow to the Solar plexus, chest plate or chin/head.

Axe Forearm

Ideal tool to break the collarbone.

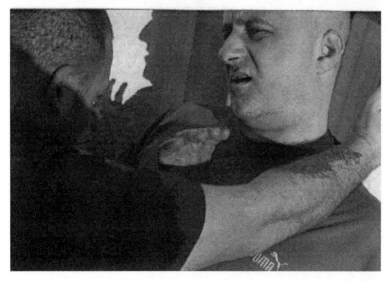

Baseball Bat

This is the bouncers 'Secret' invisible baseball bat. I never went to work without my invisible baseball bat. Absolutely devastating if directed to the neck.

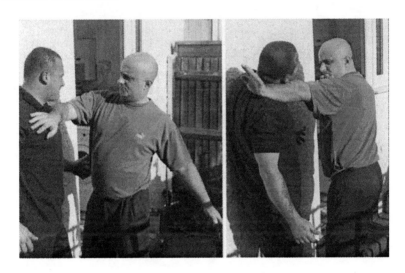

Wrist to Collar Bone

Similar to the downward forearm strike but more useful at close range if movement is restricted.

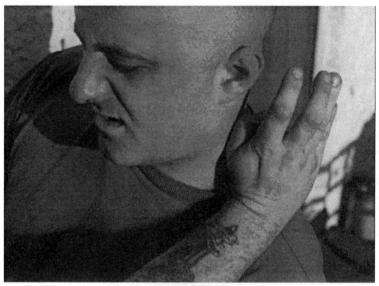

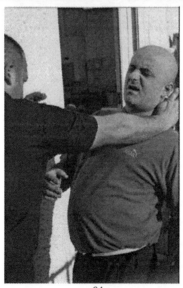

Knifehand

This classic Palm up strike is better known as the Judo chop even though such techniques never existed in Judo. It is widely practised by Karate and Kung Fu systems as a blow to the side of neck or temple.

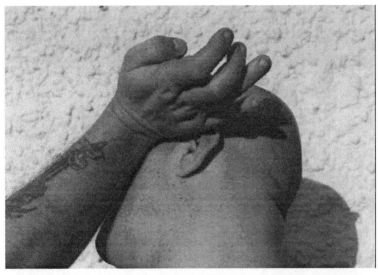

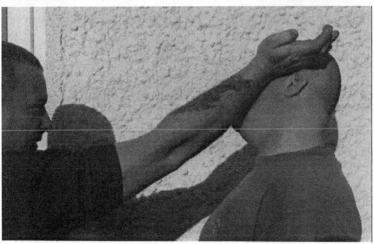

Chop

I personally find this palm down strike one of the most flowing, flexible, fastest and natural strikes that our body is capable of.

Backhand Slap

A real favourite of mine.

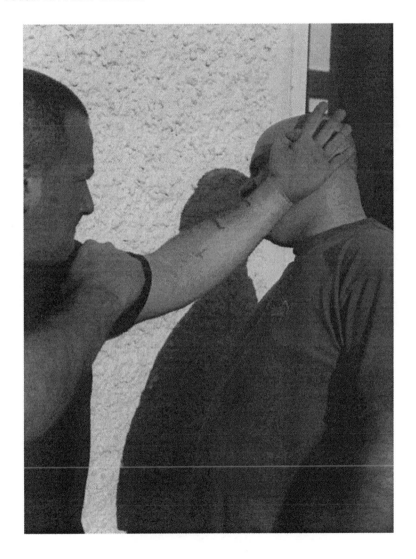

Inner-hand Slap

I have never had anybody come back at me after delivering one of these. At full speed it's a devastating blow.

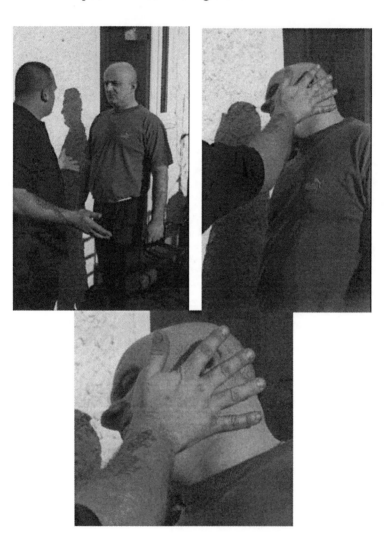

Palm Strike

Very effective to the jaw, throat, or chest plate, and ideal if you do not want to use a closed fist.

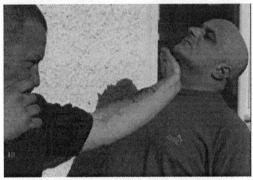

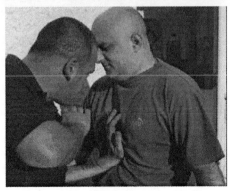

Double Slap

I absolutely love this technique when used with force to the side of neck or jaw. Many martial artists talk about doing this technique with cupped hands to burst the eardrums?

I much prefer striking as if using the flat head of two shovels, in and out, to the side of the neck rapidly, reacting as if I were placing the palm of my hands onto a red-hot iron.

Backfist

Another classic Kung fu/Karate strike which can be used pretty much in any direction, from any angle.

Hammerfist

This type of strike can be effectively used by almost anybody regardless of strength or physical ability, although a heavier force would be needed to cause a break to the collarbone.

Club Punch

A strange inner hand, type of punch which I developed for use on the door when I wanted something more solid than a slap, but could not comfortable launch a hook punch. It was developed for use in the nightclub and also resembles a wooden club, hence the name 'Club punch.'

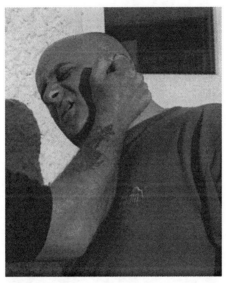

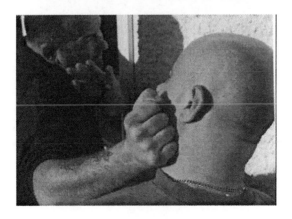

Jab

Not everybody can make his or her leading left or right jab effective enough to be considered worthy enough as a stand-alone pre-emptive strike. Make sure 'you can' if it's to be one of your pre-emptive strikes.

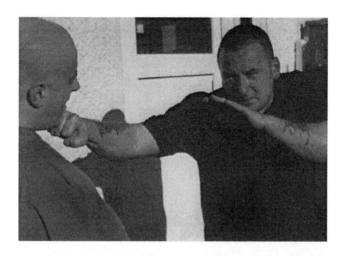

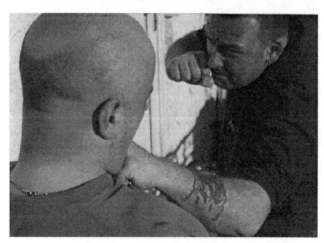

Cross

A great punch if all the elements come together at the point of impact. Even the untrained guy off the street can throw one of these to great effect. For the purposes of showing the untrained reader that the Cross is a punch from the rear arm, I have included the first photo showing the Jab, so the reader can see a difference. Otherwise the picture of the cross punch, would look like a Jab due to the angle it was taken at.

Hook

An excellent technique to launch from either the lead or rear hand.

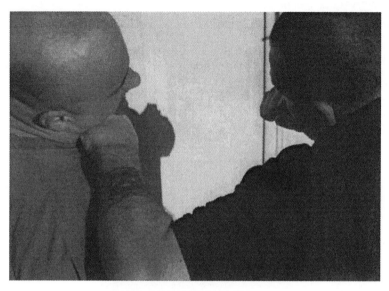

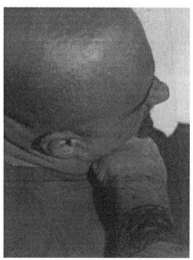

Uppercut

The underneath of the jaw was made for this punch. I once hit a guy with an uppercut, causing him to bite deep and almost through his tongue. Not a nice way to end up.

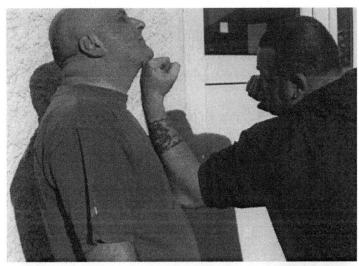

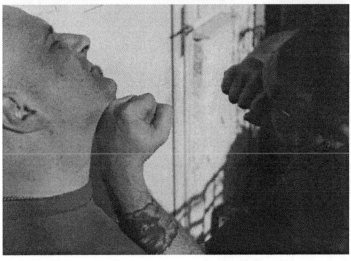

Finger Jab

If you want to feel somebody's brain, this is an open pathway. If you prefer something a little less severe then this strike to the eyes is effective against everybody. Nobody is immune to this strike.

If I had to choose just one technique from the thousands that I know, the fingertip jab to the eyes would win – hands up!

Each fingertip will make contact in or around the eye area, ensuring a good level of impact with each hand thrown out.

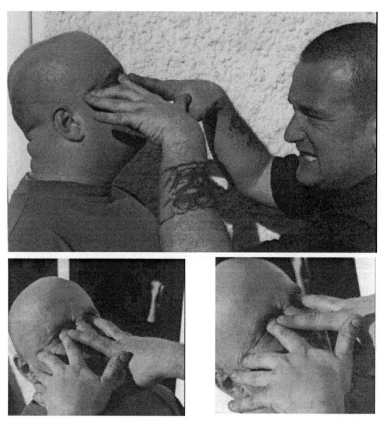

Arc Hand to Throat

Not something that would be at the top of my list but still a technique that can cause considerable damage.

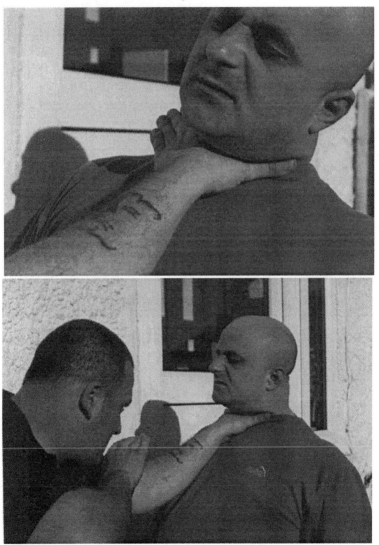

Windpipe Squeeze

Only really effective if the recipient cannot move backwards, away from the strike. If used as if trying to touch the thumb tip and fingertips at the rear of the windpipe, it will work beautifully.

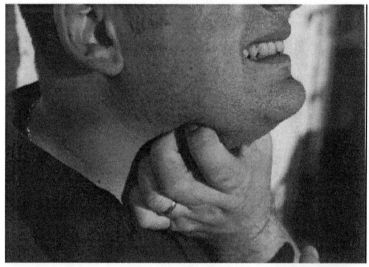

Hair Grab

I love this one when pulled hard and fast to the floor within a fraction of a second. No good though against the baldies, skinheads, or the secret wig brigade.

Head Twist

This is great for twisting the neck and can cause extreme damage to the 'Axis' vertebrae at the base of the skull.

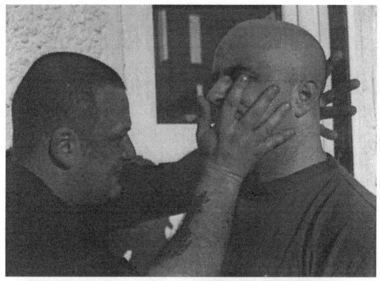

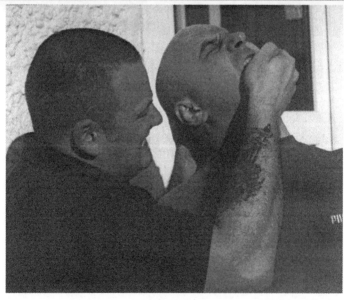

Knee

Most people would use this strike to connect to the stomach or a pulled down head. I prefer a sharp knee jab to the centreline of the chestplate. Apologies for the darkness of photo.

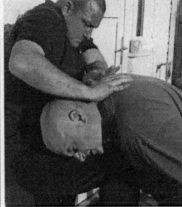

Rising Kicks

Whether snapped in with the instep or with the shin, the groin is the most obvious choice here.

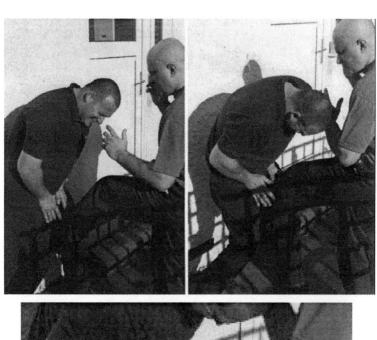

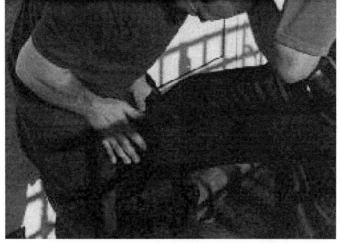

Round Kicks

I prefer the semi-locked-leg, shin to the thigh to temporarily deaden the nerves in the thigh, but also use the snap kick with instep to the knee joint or ankle to cause more serious and permanent damage, as demonstrated here by Micky. Once again, apologies for darkness of photograph.

Thrust Forward Kicks

Any type of thrusting forward kick that I do will be delivered to the pelvic bone as the point of impact, with my full body weight following behind.

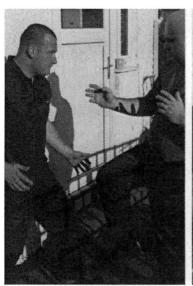 

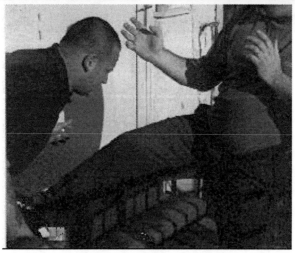

Thrust Backward Kicks

As with the front kick, I would aim for the pelvic bone and follow through with my body weight.

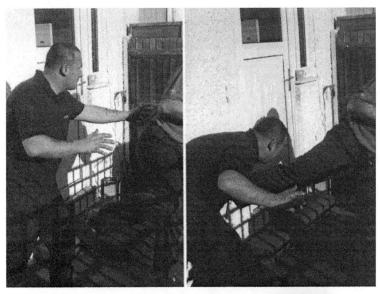

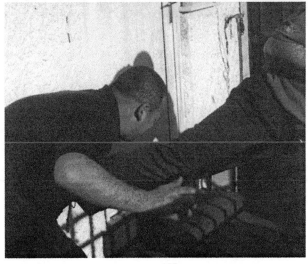

Stamping Kicks

Best done if somebody is on the floor but can also be done if they are seated and about to rise. It can also be directed towards the toes, upper foot, and shin if they are standing.

I once used this on a guys hamstring as he kneeled down to retrieve a concealed weapon from his boot. He was bluffing, I wasn't!

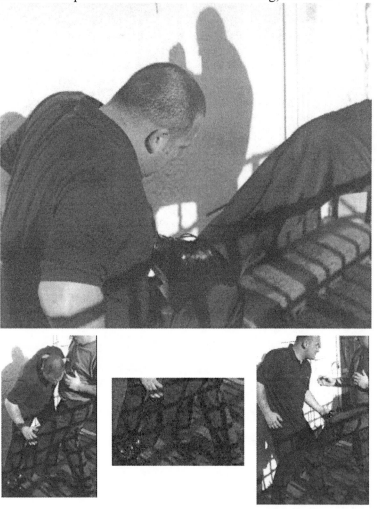

Death Stare – Visual Strike

Some people have naturally got the look, others can create it at a moments notice, and other have no hope.
If you can make it work for you as a pre-emptive strike, great. It's saved me from a physical confrontation many a time.

Oh! forgot to say – Some people are naturally ugly (above)

Verbal attack psycho strike

'Do you fucking want some? Come on then you C**t, I will tear your fucking head off'

Having an aggressive voice will help you here if you can pair it up with crazy stare and tough body language.

Not everybody is able to get the chemistry right.

Pre-emptive Strikes
With Weapons

The first and most important thing here for you to try and stay within the law is to not to use 'Weapons by design.'

What I mean by this is any item that was originally and obviously designed to be a weapon I.e. A gun, knife, stun gun, spear, sword and like. Also any item or object that has been 'adapted' to be used as a weapon. This may be something like an aluminium comb with a sharpened edge, a piece of wood cut and joined by rope or chain to act and simulate a martial arts weapon (Rice Flail), A moulded or bent piece of metal to act as a knuckle duster, along with many other things that have been adapted for use as a weapon. Anything that has been adapted or designed as a weapon is totally illegal and is likely to get you booked in at Her Majesty's Inn. So what's the answer?

The answer is contained within my book *'Dog's don't Know Kung Fu.'* It has a section dedicated to getting around this grey area of the law, but it would not be right for me to repeat it again in this book. What I will do though, is show you some things that I and other people have either used in a pre-emptive strike, or things that have been used against us in street encounters or in our guise as doormen, pre-emptively as we have approached somebody to evict them from the venue.

This information has been supplied for this book by myself and my team, consisting of doormen and self-protection professionals. I say this only to show you that the weapon attacks which follow are taken from actual real life encounters that at least one of us have experienced, either as the recipient or deliverer, and not from simulated martial arts type attacks in a safe training environment.

Look at each of the following pre-emptive strikes and ask the question,

'Is this a totally illegal weapon by design or has it been adapted or altered in any way to make it a weapon?'

or   *'Is this a normal object or item un-adapted in any way that they have used in panic to protect themselves?'*

Recognising the difference could save you from prison!

Most of the photographs illustrating weapon and empty hand pre-emptive strikes, were taken in a back garden for reasons of privacy and legality.

The people who took part are trained in both Self-protection and preservation of life. We do not endorse or suggest that you practice on training partners with the dangerous items that we have used. We have included these items for information purposes only.

For this very same reason I have not included any descriptive text to accompany the photographs. However for the less serious members of society like myself, I have left space with each one so that you can jot down some comical quotes or other ideas that each situation or weapon gives you. Although Self Protection is a serious business, please don't end up taking yourself too seriously. Enjoy your training and studies.

Forward Headbutt
Jaw-Face - Chest

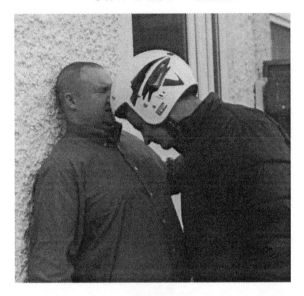

Two Fingered – Spray Attack

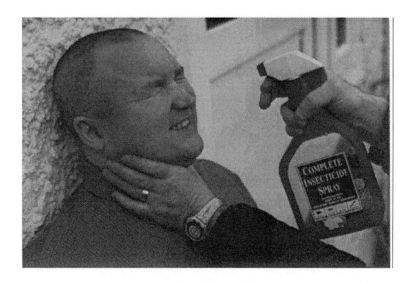

'But Doctor, the fleas have all gone now'

Forward Glass to Face

'Ah! So your glass is empty and its my round – OK I can take a hint'

Forward Round Strike with
Flattened Drink Can

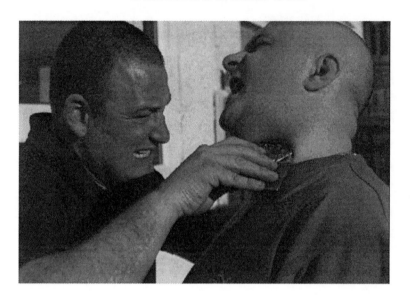

'Shaving – the Old school way'

Forward or Reverse
Bottle Neck

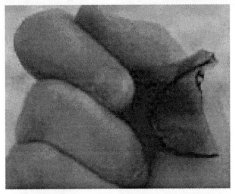

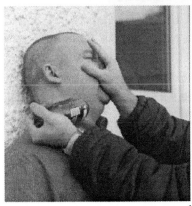 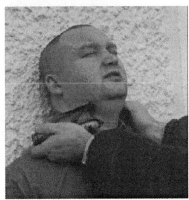

Side Weapon Jab
(Like elbow/hammer-fist to side)

Forward Metal Ruler
(As in Forward Hammer strike)

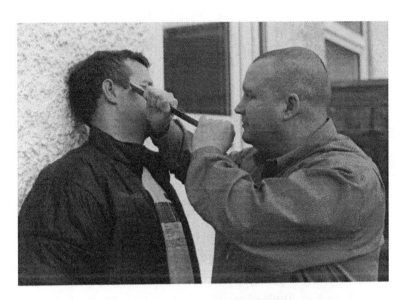

Axe Style Crash Helmet or Brick

Baseball Bat

'Jamie, honestly, I haven't seen your pork pies'

Pen Hammer-fist to Shoulder Area

Knifehand Style Strike
(Snapped credit/points card to neck)

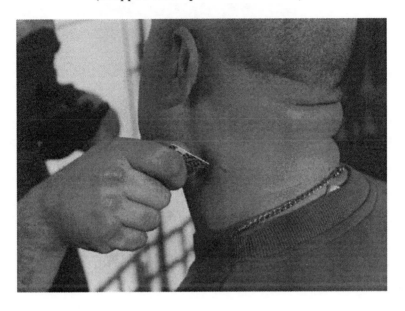

Chop/Hammer pen strike to Throat

'This pencil sharpener is shit'

Backhand, Rolled Magazine Slap

'Bloody flies'

Inner hand Dog Lead Slap

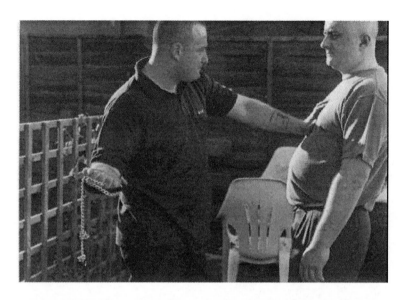

'Steve normally does this with his handbag!'

CD strike, Complete or Broken

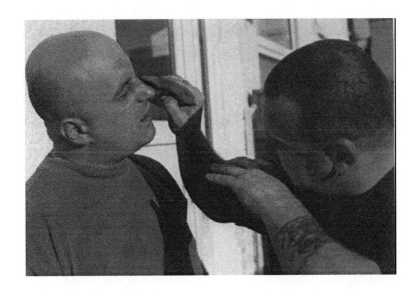

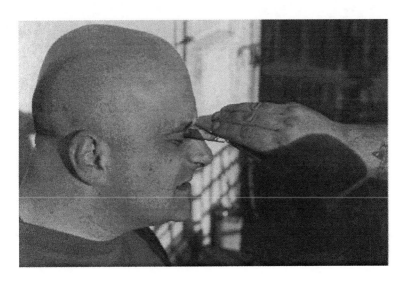

'I still can't hear anything'

Double Pen Slap

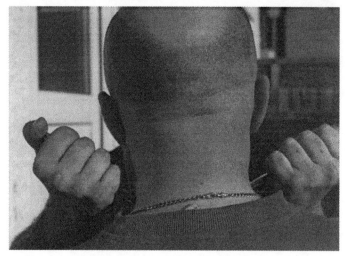

'If it was good enough for Frankenstein'

Double Slap
Two Broken Bottles

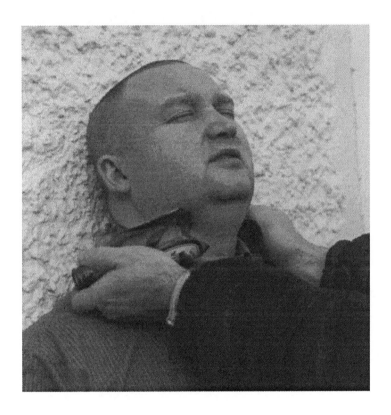

'Are you sure this will sort out my toothache'

Double Slap with Two Pairs of Scissors

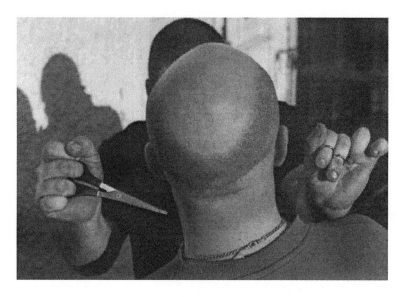

'So anyway, in 'Edward Scissor Hands' he got this guy..'

Backfist, Spring Loaded Baton

Afro Comb Hammerfist

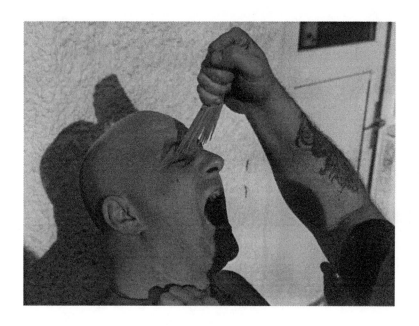

Dinner Fork Hammer Punch

Knuckle Duster to Jaw

Nicotine Enhanced
Spit to the Eyes

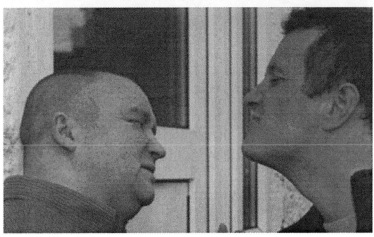

Arc Scissors Hand to Throat

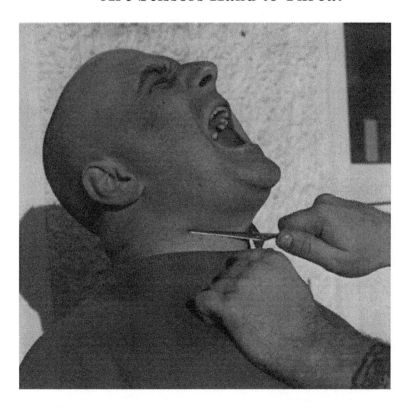

Bladed Knuckle Duster

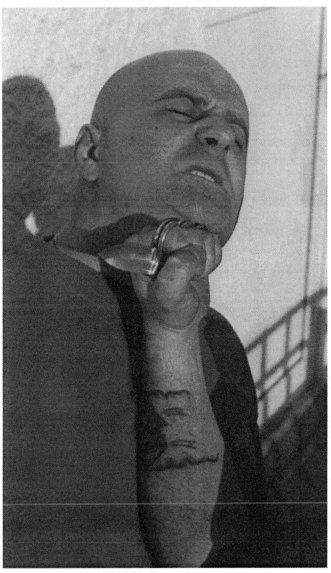

Trimming Knife

Keys Concealed in Left Hand

Double Chin Amputation
With Pruning Shears

Head Twist With Towel

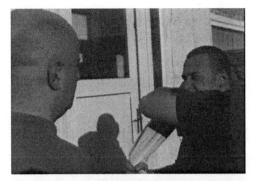

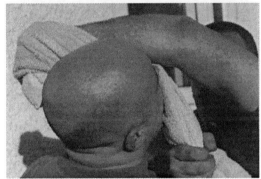

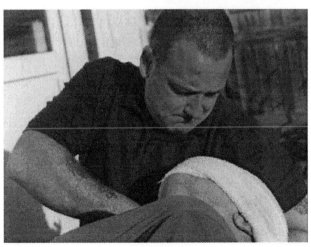

Thrust Forward Kick Door Shut

Thrust Forward Slam Door Shut

Using Wall to Smash Face

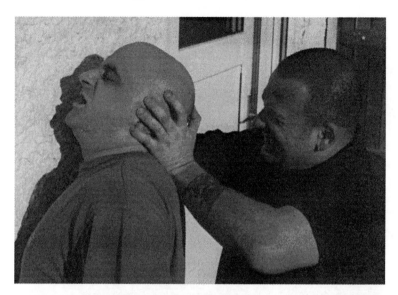

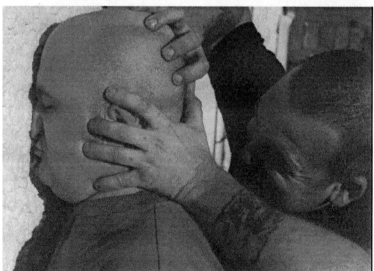

'Come on, admit you were in the Adams Family Fester'

Cup of Boiling Water to Face

Multiple Attacks

No matter how many people you feel like fighting today, try to stick to fighting one at a time, because I don't care how good you think you are, one pair of hands and feet cannot deal with three pairs of hands and feet. Basic mathematics will tell you that.

Take a look at a Juggler. Even though he appears to be dealing with three to five balls with only two hands, he is only really holding one or two balls at a time. *(I think I should have re-phrased this).* To fight more than one person, you too will have to be like the Juggler and move with precision and speed to get your timing just right in order to make contact to each person with your combination of pre-emptive blows.

That's the only way that you can do it, no matter what anybody else has told you.

If you miss the opportunity to juggle your strikes and stop the multiple attack, you will certainly not be able to avoid the next stage which will be a combination of being grappled, taken to the floor and severely beaten.

Weapon Attacks

I still firmly believe that the martial arts do not have a solution to knife attacks and other edged weapons, and only go part way in their advice on how to deal with such encounters. For an in-depth study of how I deal with weapon attacks read my book 'Dogs don't know kung fu'

What I will say here is that you will either have been hit with a weapon because it was cleverly concealed, or you were switched off. In which case it's a bit late for your pre-emptive strike.

The other scenario is that you get a glimpse of a weapon because you 'were' switched on, or the holder of the weapon has made it known to you that they have a weapon.

Any type of instrument that could possible be used against you, to cause harm, will have a warning label on it.

It is very tiny and invisible to the naked eye, but believe me it's there. It reads,

' *The holder of this weapon is about to take a diabolical liberty with you and intends on causing you to suffer with this instrument. Please stop this person from breaking the law by giving them a beating that they will never forget. Please remember that you feared for your safety*'

I'm sure that's what it says!

War Stories

Pre-emptive strikes almost always win the day whether used by you, or against you. Yet many people still stupidly believe that their knowledge and ability of blocking will keep them safe from the reality of the sudden un-announced pre-emptive strike.
It won't!

I am going to include a few short stories that involve either myself, or people I know, or have worked with, to show you different ways in which the pre-emptive strike has been used, for, or against them.
The stories that I have included are all true without any bells or whistles added in order to not make a hero of anybody or glorify violence.
I call this little collection of tales 'War stories.'

The Three Unwise Men

It was the middle of summer around four years ago and as usual I collected my three children from their home for my once weekly access. I had been working the door all-night and arrived home tired, cold, and bored and had only 4 hours sleep before I went to collect the children. I do not handle tiredness well and do tend to snap at the slightest push. I don't mean physically, but I will be the first to admit that I am hard to tolerate when I'm tired. However I look forward so much to having my kids for the day that I try my hardest to put on a loving smile and be everything I can, and should be, as a father.

I took my children out for the day, which helped to keep me awake, and would also be enjoyable for them. I tried my hardest to not be around other adults because I knew that I could easily get into a disagreement about stupid immaterial things due to tiredness lowering my tolerance. This unfortunately was part and parcel of being a doorman, It destroys your social communication with those that are closest to you, like friends and family. Being with the children all day within their little world, would bring me back to reality world, away from the door environment, which I sometimes 'thought' was the real world. My day with my children was, and still is, a very special time for me, and I try my hardest to not let anybody, or anything spoil that.

That day I decided to take my children to the Zoo at Colchester. We planned to spend the complete day there having fun until closing time, and then take a slow drive home. Halfway through the day we went to watch the 'bird of prey' display. I think it was a Kestrel and Falcon doing stunts. Sitting behind we were three lads aged around eighteen who were obviously under the influence of alcohol. They were sitting there being loud, rude and generally making a nuisance of themselves.

One of them made a remark about one of the birds shitting on a girl's head as it flew over. People were trying their best to ignore them but I was finding it hard to ignore.

I turned around and asked the lads to calm down, I said,

'People are trying to watch the show, will you please be quiet.'

The nosiest one of the three put a little show on for his pals by making out that he was going to go for me, but also, at the same time, letting his mates hold him back. I decided to avoid further conflict and move on, and not watch the rest of the show.

I would have been too vulnerable sitting back down with my back to them. I also did not want to get into any trouble or fights whilst I had my children with me. As we were walking away one of my children said,

'*Dad, those horrible men are following us,*' I replied,

'*Don't be silly, this is the way everybody comes out, let's go over to the ball pond.*' (I knew we were being followed.)

This was an enclosed area where children could play indoors in a pool of plastic balls, use climbing frames, and so on, whilst being supervised by some of the zoo staff. I asked one of the helpers if they could keep an eye on the three little ones, along with my eldest son who was around 13 years old (he's 18 now), so that I could go to the toilet. It was quite clear to me that the three loudmouth lads were following us as a form of intimidation. I wanted to put a stop to them trying to spoil my day. I walked over to the water fountain to make sure that I was within their sights and then made my way over to the toilet area. I just wanted to tell them to get the fuck out of my face otherwise I would call for the police. The lads approached me and just looked, laughed and whispered. As I approached them I caught half a giggling whisper that made reference to the large birthmark that the girl in front of them had on her head, and also suggesting that

it may have been birds shit. It dawned on me that they were referring to my little girl, who at the time did have a very disguising birthmark on her forehead. Its not something that I really noticed much because it was just one of her natural features which has now virtually disappeared and has become unnoticeable as she grew older. It is way before this stage that I should have used the art of prediction and thought about the  consequences of what could happen to me if I got involved in an argument.

My children were expecting me back in a minute; I had to get them home trouble free, and so on. However, today I couldn't fight it, and made the wrong choice. I let go with a left hook punch to the jaw of idiot who made the comment about my daughter, putting him out for the count. The other two just froze, which gave me the opportunity to go to work with my verbal assault. I can be a silver-tongued devil at times.

They obviously denied the insults, remarks and intimidation as they helped their mate up, who was still catching up on some sleep. Is strange how when people think that you are about to beat their brains in that they want to tell you their life story. It turned out that they were army boys from the local garrison out on a days leave getting pissed and just enjoying themselves. Their mistake was that they tried to do it at my daughter's expense. Very unwise. Although I don't think that they had intended getting physical with me, I believe that they would have continued to try intimidating me, which in turn would scare my children. To me this amounts to a common assault, which I responded to. I acted wrongly according to the prediction process, wrong in the eyes of the law and wrong as a responsible parent, but I felt better for doing it. What would you have done in this situation if you were in my position? Would you have reported the lads at to a zoo official after leaving the bird display? Would you have launched a pre-emptive strike at the first encounter, whilst seated at the show? Would you have left the zoo quickly and gone home? Or would you have carried on walking ignoring the fact that you were being followed?

My choice was due to bullshit male bravado and anger. I knew exactly why I tried to gain their attention and draw them over to the toilet area. I was hoping to find any excuse I could to confront them, where we would be out of view from witnesses and of course, my children. Have a real good think about how you would have handled it?

Pride or Body

Pride is a strange thing! We protect it like we would our car or home and in most cases would put it at to the top of the list, if that position weren't firmly taken by the protection of our loved ones. We tend to put the protection of our pride way in front of the protection of our own body. The problem with defending our pride is that it clouds our judgement of right and wrong, danger and safety, law abiding or law breaking, comfort or pain along with many other things.

As a youngster defending my pride came before any danger, harm, pain or abiding by the law of the land. I was immature but proud of the fact that I would defend my pride at all cost.

Here's a little tale of defending ones pride.

I was around fifteen years old and just beginning to get to grips with the martial arts. I had been doing Judo for a few years and was now pursuing my interest in Karate. I was not a good fighter but was getting into schoolboy fights every single day. The sheer amount of fights that I was having dictated that sooner or later I would have to win. Unfortunately, winning a fight also gives you that false sense of feeling that you are a fighter. I was not, but I'm sure that I was beginning to think that I was.

One day I was waiting for a bus with two friends of mine when a car approached us. The car had five skinhead lads in it who for some reason were out to randomly set upon innocent people and beat them up.

They began using intimidating stares to inject some fear into us but even without that we were scared. We were in a remote area with the nearest house some distance away.

The skinheads made it clear that they wanted us to run so that they could play Fox and Hound with us, chasing us with the car. We stood there hoping that a distant view of a bus would appear, but today that was not happening for us.

As the passenger door opened we knew that a beating was on today's menu. As the first guy got out my two pals bolted off in opposite directions. My pride would not let me run.

As much as I wanted the earth to swallow me up and hide me away from this ugly encounter, I just stood and stared. I was absolutely shitting myself.

The five lads were now around me and I knew my beating was soon to follow, but for some reason I still hoped for a last minute interruption to their plan. I had stupidly not used my chance of escape wisely and was now going to pay for it.

I felt the thud of the lump of wood sink into my skull, followed by the steel toecap boots, fists, and other weapons.

I ended up in hospital with my skull cracked open, broken arm and wrist, and looked like a bruised apple all because my pride stopped me from pre-empting their attack by running away.

Running away is a form of pre-emptive measure that you can take in order to avoid the pain and suffering of a violent attack.

I stupidly chose to protect my pride rather than my body. I knew that I could not possibly win an encounter with five guys, with or without them having weapons. All I can put this day down to was pride affecting my judgement.

'I say that you should let someone hurt your pride rather than let them hurt your body.'

Bouncers Defence

A door supervisor's job is hard enough but even harder if you are trying to be professional.

'W.H.' was a very handy guy who could look after himself, and others if the situation arose. He just wanted to do his nights work without any unnecessary encounters, however sometimes you will get the odd idiot that want's to push their luck.

At the pub it was the usual situation where customers were not allowed to take their drinks outside, off the premises, for both reasons of safety and also breach of licensing law.

'W.H.' had been in the back of the pub and was now due to take cover on the main door. When he arrived he saw a young lad having a tiff with a girl - they also had their drinks with them. 'W.H.' politely said to the couple,

'Will you please take your drinks inside, the management do not allow alcohol or glasses to be taken off the premises, we are not licensed for off sales,'

The young lad replied,

'In a minute, we are sorting something out,'

'W.H.' then politely said,

'You can stay out here as long as you like, no problem, but I must ask you to put your glasses inside the pub'

With that the young lad made a move towards W.H and snarled,

'Come on then, if you think you're a big hard bouncer, fucking make me,'

As the lad came within range of being able to 'glass' W.H., a right cross promptly stopped him. W.H. threw the pre-emptive strike to the lads jaw as he rushed forward. The lad dropped to the floor. For the people just arriving at the pub and all those looking out from inside the pub, all they could see was a lad knocked out by the bouncer. The reality of it is that the doorman had to make this move in order to protect himself. In my opinion, his actions were justified within law and under the Health and Safety act. A pre-emptive strike possibly stopped a scarred face and loss of eyesight.

Do You Know Who I Am?

Bruce Willis was taking a break from filming to do a shortstop handful of secret gigs with his band in London. I was hired to do his V.I.P. security and ensure that nobody made their way into his personal space. He was also very paranoid about anyone taking photos of him and pointing things towards him.

With someone as high profile as Bruce Willis, who was standing centre stage in this tiny little club, within arms reach of a couple of hundred people, it was not an easy nights work. In theory it should be trouble free because the majority of the audience were by invitation only, like record company people, other celebrities etc but you still always get the odd person slip through on somebody else's guest list. This is where you have more chance of unpredictable behaviour shining through, from an individual.

A small section of the club was roped off and had three tables and chairs reserved for Mick Jagger, and a few other celebrities who were due to arrive for the show.

The venue manager came to the dressing room where I was looking after Bruce and asked me to deal with a situation. Some guy had sat himself down at one of the tables within the reserved area and nobody seemed to know who he was. He was a big lump who reminded me very much of the Rock singer Meatloaf because of his clothing, size and hair, but it wasn't him.

I approached the guy and said,

'*Excuse me sir, this is a reserved area, do you have a pass to be here?*' knowing full well that he hadn't, because I knew all the stars that were to be seated there. He slowly lifted up his head and stared through me replying,

'*Don't you fucking know who I am?*' I thought shit! I'm going to make myself look a right fool here I don't recognise him; I didn't have a clue who he was. I said,

'*I do apologise but I don't recognise you, or know who you are, what's your name?*' he came back with,

'*Demi Moore*'

He was a crank, a looney tune.

That's the last thing I needed, a nutter on the premises.

'Get up and get the fuck out of here' I replied as I pointed to the exit. The looney said,

'My husband is Bruce Willis and he is expecting me, I'm not going anywhere.'

With that I took my pen from my jacket sleeve and used it along with my thumb tip as a pinching device to the guys ear, in order to help him to his feet. He was too heavy for me to be able to pull up, so in situations like this I prefer to use some tools of my trade, which help out when I have a problem. These secret little methods of applying condensed pain to somebody are described in my books 'Old school-New School' and 'Dogs don't know kung fu.' They are great attitude adjusters.

Anyway, with the help of my pre-emptive pinch to the guy's ear, I easily escorted him out of the building. I spoke to the doorman of the club and said,

'Who let that clown in the club?,' knowing full well it must have been him. He said,

'I did, he was on the guest list'

'Show me' I said,

He pointed to it and said,

'There it is, his name is Demi Moore'

I looked at him in amazement and said,

'You prick, don't you fucking know who Demi Moore is?'

He obviously didn't.

Who knows what the cranky guy was up to? I just hope that that my pre-emptive ear pinch put a stop to the crazy guy's intention, whatever it may have been.

Bruce kindly thanked me for protecting his life by buying me a new house, car and my very own speedboat, (Yeah right!).

The Bully and the Joker

There are many occasions that you will not want to get into a fight because of factors that do not normally get considered when discussing self-protection.

Some that come to mind are the £400 suit that you are wearing because you have a special engagement or interview, your late for something, You are ill, you realise you are in the wrong, you simply want to avoid hurting someone or getting hurt yourself, and so on. There are 1,001 reasons that you just do not want to get into a fight today, even if you know that you can pulverise the person who is in your face.

Gary, a good friend of mine, was into weight training and martial arts and had trained with me for years. He is pleasant, well mannered and likes to make people laugh. Although he is very capable of taking care of himself, it's near on impossible to upset him.

Gary was at a friend's party just having the usual laugh and joke when one guy took a dislike to him. Gary is no fool, and knows when somebody is having a dig at him. He could feel this guy making eye contact with him but he did not want to make an issue of it, understanding that alcohol was probably the cause of the problem here. He went into the kitchen to get some food when the guy approached him and said,

'*Don't I know you,*' as he drew on his cigarette and blew it out into Gary's direction.

'*I don't think so*' Gary replied, '*my parents don't normally allow me out this late.*' This was his humorous way of saying, just go away and play tough guy with someone else. Gary was about 30 years old so obviously wasn't under a time curfew by his parents, but the guy wasn't amused. He came back with,

'*Yeah I remember where I know you from, it was the nick, wasn't it?*' Gary was far to advanced at this game, to get drawn in to a situation that easily. I had also trained him well in sarcasm .

'*Were you the one that nicked my sandwiches in the staff canteen?*' Gary replied.

A few of the girls at the party were laughing at the way this guy was being played with by Gary. He angrily said,

'*No, I was on the other side, I was a con,*' and with that he did the classic Bruce Lee stance and continued,

'*These hands are lethal, you want to watch yourself, I'm a second Dan brown belt*'

Gary who could easily have taken the guy apart but being the type of person he is, said,

'*Wow, put those hands away, are they loaded, that Kung fu stuff frightens me, I don't want to get involved in all that*' as he made out to back away. As Gary jumped in a backwards direction making out he was scared of the guy, the bully began making the classic Bruce Lee high pitched martial art sounds as he was waving his arms all over the place, simulating Kung fu moves, rather poorly.

The guy then proud of his display of 'Fighting – without fighting' walked out from the kitchen with his chest puffed out, swaying his shoulders like someone who had just gained a victory. Everybody was laughing at him but he was so wrapped up in his own ego that he couldn't see it. Little did he know that Gary was one of my 2nd Dan's who would have taken him to pieces with no trouble at all, but rather, he chose to let him go. Gary was having a good time chilling out at the party and that day, he just didn't want to get into a fight.

Some week's later Gary was at the local nightclub where he had gone to visit his pals, who just happen to be the doormen there. The night was going smoothly when suddenly Gary heard a voice from behind him,

'*Oy Rambo, remember me,*'

It was the guy from the party, but this time he was with his mates and was intent on taking things just that little bit further, putting a little show on for his pals. The guy said,

'*I want you to buy a drink for me and my mates,*'

whilst using aggressive body language and pointing his finger so that from the distance it looked to his friends that he was giving Gary a right telling off.

He then walked back over to his mates to soak up the glory of being a tough guy, and to tell his mates that free drinks were on their way.

The bouncer said to Gary,

'*I will kick him out for you*,' but Gary replied,

'*No, let me deal with it, here, hold my drink for me.*'

Gary knew it was time to nip this situation in the bud and made his way over to the group of lads.

As the loudmouth went to further his display of bullying, Gary pre–emptively hit the guy with a double palm heel push, knocking him over and forcing him backwards, sliding across the floor.

As the bully looked up from the floor in gutted shock, Gary pointed at him and said,

'*Next time keep your guard up!*'

That was the end of that.

Unfortunately, because Gary did not deal with the guy at the time of the party. The bully took it as a sign of weakness, as if Gary was scared, and the Guy decided to milk the situation a little more.

The bully came unstuck .....

False Sense of Security

From the day I enrolled into the martial arts, one of the dreams I had was to become a black belt. Of course, I wanted to be able to fight and look after myself as well, but to be able to say that I was a black belt gave me a great feeling inside.

Becoming a black belt is like a lottery win. Some people handle it with care and other use it foolishly. I came into the second category. I was young and immature.

The black belt did not disappear from my waist once I physically took it off after a training session. An imaginary black belt would remain in its place just like 'The King's new clothes', if you know that fable.

I could see and feel the black belt hanging around my waist, but I was alone on this, nobody else could see it, for the obvious reason that it was a figment of my imagination.

It was so crazy. A situation would occur somewhere, be it a pub, burger bar, shopping centre or sitting on a tube, and I would immediately switch on inside, ready to get myself involved in some way. Once again, nobody else was aware of it because nothing was really happening; it was all happening in my mind. I would stand there and look at whoever it was causing a disturbance and send a message within my thoughts and eyes saying '*I'm a black belt, don't mess with me.*'

I was obviously the only one that was aware of my thoughts being sent out because it was happening in my own little world, inside my head. The only thing that other people could see was a nosey person trying to see what was going on. They could not see any imaginary black belt hanging around my waist or martial techniques flashing through my mind.

You may think that my disclosure of the above is a little unusual, but every martial artist has experienced this and I would think that every holder of the black belt automatically goes through this, even subconsciously, whenever an eruption occurs. On this particular day I was waiting at a bus stop, for a bus to arrive. I was going into town to get some bits. I was around 20 years old then and pretty much in my prime of fitness and Martial arts ability.

Two lads were asking people at the bus stop if they had a spare cigarette. If a cigarette was not handed over they then asked for money to buy some. One of the people near to me was an old guy who wasn't taking this intimidation from the lad lightly and challenged them.

'Why don't you bugger off. You shouldn't smoke if you can't afford to buy your own. Now piss off, out of it,' he said,

The lads weren't impressed with the old guys comments and began bad mouthing him.

I stepped in to help save the old guy from a possible beating. I felt that being a black belt was going to be enough to stop their actions and they would be frightened away when they realised that my hands were 'lethal.'

The lads did not see a Karate black belt or martial artist challenging them, all they could see was a skinny lad daring to challenge the pair of them. (Yes! I was skinny once).

My reward was a pre-emptive headbutt from one of them, turning my eyes into water fountains, followed up by a swift kick in the bollocks!

I curled up on the pavement in agony as they ran of laughing and taunting me.

The false sense of security that my imaginary black belt gave me, quickly introduced me to the laws of reality in the form of a pre-emptive strike.

That lesson has stayed with me for the last seventeen years. The skinniness didn't!

Final Words!

I really do hope that this book has made you think differently about the concept of the pre-emptive strike, and when you should use it.

To train it thoroughly you must firstly be able to store and have easy access to your techniques. My 'head to toe system ©' will assist you there. Once this is sorted and you have an arsenal of weaponry to choose from, you must then narrow this down to a few pre-emptive strikes that 'take care of business' for you.

When you have these chosen strikes, you must 'Sharpen the saw', in other words, keep the techniques sharp, fast and effective.

Do this by practising on punch bags, hand held pads or other impact training devices that you currently use. Two things though – Don't practice your fingertip jabs, headbutts, elbows etc against anything too solid, i.e. a brick wall. The damage it will cause to you is obvious. Rather, try to do it against something that is closer to the feeling of hitting a real person. You do not have to go to the extreme measures of hitting hanging carcasses like the late great 'Lenny McLean' did in his pre-fight training. However you can find a compromise by using heavy bags or getting a training partner to hold impact pads for you.

One of my personal methods is to get a training partner to hold two tomatoes at eye level, so that I can simulate my fingertip pre-emptive jab. When I'm happy that my strike can penetrate the tomatoes and cause discomfort to the palm of my training partner's hand, I know I've got it! The eye sockets are the only way into the brain without cracking open the skull.

For the headbutt I use an old car tyre-inner tube, filled with talcum powder. This is like a very large version of the 'Stress balls' that you can buy in the high street. You even see them on keyrings now so that people can squeeze them to un-stress.

This should set you off on ways to use training aids. To further assist you I will be releasing a book and video on the subject later on in 2000.

One thing that I do advise against is striking out to the empty air as a shadow boxer would. A full blast, fast pre-emptive strike to thin air could be damaging to your joints and in my opinion serves no purpose. It gives a different feel to your strikes, which is unnatural and false.

There is no point whatsoever striking out at nobody!

When was the last time you were threatened or attacked by 'nobody'?

So there you have it...
'Pre-emptive Strikes for Winning Fights'

Take on board my advice and get the best from your current system of training and other sources to aid you in the fight for self-protection.

Stay safe on the streets!

Jamie O'Keefe
December 1998

The End

Grappling for Reality

If you want to learn grappling from those that practice what they preach, here are some people that we suggest you try out.
Each instructor has been personally endorsed by Jamie O'Keefe as superb grappling Instructors.

Dave Turton 7th Dan   Tel/Fax: 01709 710489
The Self-Defence Federation
Grappling & Self Protection
Clubs in Rotherham, Batley
Monday – Wednesday – Thursday

Darrin Richardson Tel: 01705 352972
Sambo wrestling and Ju-Jitsu
Classes in Gosport, Hampshire.

Kevin O'Hagan   Tel: 0117 9525711
Grappling. Ju-jitsu, & Self Protection
Classes in Bristol

Lee Hasdell   Tel: 01908 255534
Total Fight Forum
4th Floor Exchange House
494 Midsummer Boulevard
Central Milton Keynes

Combat
Magazine

Self Protection
Column in
each issue by
Jamie O'Keefe

Available from
Temple Publishing
Tel: 0121 3443737
And all newsagents

Adverts

Will the reader please note that the following advertising section of the book is included to let you know of other Self Protection related merchandise.

You the reader, have not been charged for the printing or paper used in this section. The cost for this has been absorbed by New Breed Publishing.

The price that you have paid for this publication is for the knowledge, information and advice given by Jamie O'Keefe throughout the rest of this book.

Email

books@newbreed.worldonline.co.uk

www.newbreedbooks.co.uk

**Other books that are a must
For your collection**

Read about the 20th Century

Read about the 20th Century
'Secret - self protection weapon'
also
Everything you need to know about
EDGED WEAPONS
in
'Dogs don't know Kung fu'
By Jamie O'Keefe

THE BEST BOOK EVER WRITTEN
PREVENT YOURSELF FROM BECOMING A VICTIM
'Dogs don't know Kung Fu'

A guide to Female Self Protection
By Jamie O'Keefe **£ 14** inclusive P&p

Never before has Female Self Protection used this innovative approach to pose questions like. Why do Rapist's Rape? Why are Women abused? Why do Stalkers Stalk? This book takes a look at all Simple, Serious, and Life threatening aspects of Self Protection that concern us daily, along with **PREVENTION** of Child abuse and Child Abduction, Emotional cruelty, Telephone abuse, Road rage, Muggers, Date rape, Weapon attacks, Female abduction, Sexual Assault & Rape, Self defence law, and what it will allow us to do to protect ourselves, plus much more. With over 46,500 words, 77 pictures and 200 printed pages "Dog's Don't Know Kung fu" is a no nonsense approach to women's self defence. It covers many realistic scenarios involving Children's abduction as well as typical attacks on women. Besides quoting actual events, the book explains how to avoid trouble and how you should react if you get into a situation.

This book is a 'must read' for all women and parents.

It is also important for teenage women, but, due to some of its graphic depiction's of certain incidences, parents should read it first and decide if it's suitable for their child.

What Makes Tough Guys Tough?
The Secret Domain

WHAT MAKES

TOUGH GUYS
TOUGH
The Secret Domain
by Jamie O'Keefe

Written by Jamie O'Keefe

Jamie O'Keefe has interviewed key figures from Boxing, Martial arts, Self Protection, Bodyguards, Doorwork, Military, Streetfighting and so on. Asking questions that others were too polite to ask but secretly wanted to know the answers.

Interviews include Peter Consterdine, Geoff Thompson, and Dave Turton from the countries leading Self Protection organisation 'The British Combat Association.'

Along with Boxing heroes Dave 'Boy' Green and East London's former Commonwealth Champion Mo Hussein.

Plus unsung heroes from the world of Bouncers, Foreign Legion, Streetfighters, and more.

This book also exposes the Secret Domain, which answers the question 'What makes tough guys tough.'

Find out what some of the toughest guys on the planet have to say about 'What makes tough guys tough' and how they would turn you into a tough guy.

Thugs, Mugs and Violence
The story so far

In this true account of his journey, Jamie O'Keefe unveils the reality of living in the East End of London. From childhood to adult this compelling, harrowing and often highly amusing story tells of his encounters with street fighting, crime, drugs, violence and the martial arts. It goes through the trials and tribulations of boyhood right through to his days of working on the door in the heart of London's nightlife. Read how each of his confrontations and experiences have played a major part in making him the well respected authority in the fighting arts that he is today.

This book is sure to intrigue and fascinate you so much it will be hard to put it down..

"Jamie's book 'Thugs, Mugs and violence' is an insight into the violent times of today and should be read"
Reg Kray 'Kray Twins'

Photograph kindly supplied to Jamie for inclusion by

**REG KRAY
32 YEARS SERVED
1968 – 2000
HM Prison.
R.I.P.**

THUGS, MUGS
and
VIOLENCE

An Autobiography
By
Jamie O'Keefe

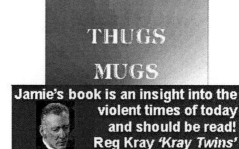

One mans encounter with Thugs, Mugs and Violence
as a Bouncer, Martial Artist, Streetfighter and former East end
gang member.
A fascinating book that will introduce you to
Life's hidden world of drugs, guns, violence,
and revenge.

£14 inc p&p
from NEW BREED
Po box 511, Dagenham Essex RM9 5DN

THUGS, MUGS
and
VIOLENCE

REVIEWED AS
'BOOK OF THE MONTH'
Front magazine

£14 inc p&p
from NEW BREED
Po box 511, Dagenham Essex RM9 5DN

Kevin O'Hagans latest book
BAD TO THE BONE
Exploring the many facets of violence
and aggressive behaviour

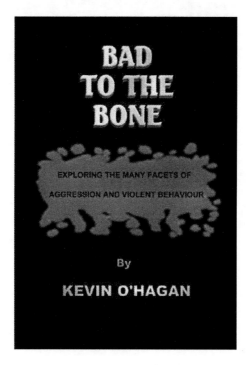

£14 inc Post and packing
from New Breed, Po box 511
Dagenham, Essex RM9 5DN

FROM BULLIED TO BLACK BELT
BY SIMON MORRELL
from
New Breed, Po box 511
Dagenham, Essex RM9 5DN
£ 14 inc Post and packing

Please feel free to review any of our books on
www.amazon.co.uk

Why not also look at the dedicated websites of the
New Breed Authors
Jamie O'Keefe
www.newbreedbooks.co.uk

Kevin O'Hagan
www.bristolgoshinjutsu.com

Alan Charlton
www.spa.ukf.net

Steve Richards
www.renaissance-academy.com

Simon Morrell
www.frombulliedtoblackbelt.net

www.blackbeltkarate.net

Steve Richards

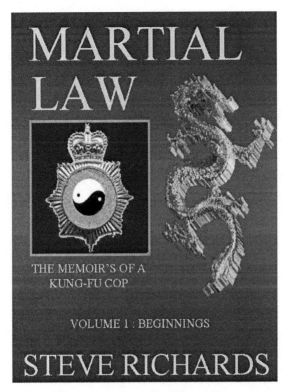

The memoirs of a Kung Fu cop
Part One – Beginnings

Topics include death, sex, serious injury, romance, pathos, tragedy, humour, riots, IRA, drugs, bouncers, getting planted and just about everything you'd expect from a Scouse Copper over 13 years front line duty. Also, loads on traditional Chinese arts from within their closed shop community, and how they worked or otherwise under real pressure. The post-police part of the book covers his martial arts and other careers since that time

£ 14 inclusive of P&P Available from
New Breed, Po box 511, Dagenham, Essex RM9 5DN

NEW BREED PUBLISHING

Would you like to train to be a Door Supervisor?

We are the only training company recommended by NEW BREED and run courses for Jamie O'Keefe on a monthly basis.

If you would like to attend one of our courses approved by Westminster, Kent and Dacorum to becoming a licensed door supervisor please give us a call to discuss your requirements.

Our courses are held in Central London but we can also arrange for them to be held at your location either in the U.K. or overseas.

If you read and enjoyed the Jamie O'Keefe book
'Old School – New school'
Then our course will suit you.

For further information please call **A.S.P. Security & Training**

On 07973 684 223
www.doorsupervisors.co.uk

Or write to

A.S.P.
92 Mottisfont road
Abbey Wood
London
SE2 9LN
* Please mention where you saw this advert

The latest book by Jamie O'Keefe
Out now

NO ONE FEARS
WHEN ANGRY!
The Psychology of
CONFRONTATION

Roy 'Pretty Boy' Shaw
And
Jamie O'Keefe
(Photo taken from book)

£14 inclusive of P&P
If you have bought a book from New Breed before
You will be automatically informed
when this book is released

A new video from Kevin O'Hagan
'DOWN AND OUT' Vol 2

More dynamic Strikes, throws and submission techniques.

Learn advanced combinations, joint locks, leg locks, chokes, strangles, and much more. This tape is loaded with first class technique.

Modern Combat Jujitsu at its best

Price £15 inclusive of Post and Packing
Contact Kevin O'Hagan for more details.
Due out now

* Please mention where you saw this advert

IMPACT JUJUTSU Vol 1

**If you are serious about improving your
All round fighting skills and conditioning,
Then this video is for you.**

**Learn 'Secret' skills for better striking,
Throwing and grappling
Plus many unique fitness and conditioning drills!**

* Please mention where you saw this advert

www.newbreedbooks.co.uk

IMPACT JUJUTSU Vol 1

by

Kevin O'Hagan, 5th Dan

(Kempo Goshin Jujutsu)

Learn dynamic drills, techniques and conditioning for realism
Through this combat Ju-Jutsu video.
'Loaded with vital information'
This tape is a must for anybody serious about training for peak fitness
and reality training skills.
Enjoy and learn from this informative and exciting new video
available **only** from Kevin O'Hagan.
Excellent value at **£ 14.00**
(Please add £ 1.00 for postage and packing)
Please make cheques payable to '**Kevin O'Hagan'**
and post to
23 Chester road, Bristol BS5 7AX

Telephone: 0117-9525711

* Please mention where you saw this advert

www.newbreedbooks.co.uk

'FISTFUL OF DYNAMITE'

**Yawara-Bo is an excellent and compact little weapon
That can be an instant source of painful control.**

**Anybody of any age can learn how to use this
Lethal little stick, quickly with good effect!**

BRISTOL GOSHIN JUTSU COMBAT ACADEMY
PRESENTS

NEW VIDEO RELEASES FOR 2000

Featuring Kevin O'Hagan 5th Dan

"FISTFUL OF DYNAMITE"
YAWARA-BO TECHNIQUES

60 mins of dynamic techniques using this small but
highly effective weapon...plus substitute makeshift
Yawara-bo's from everyday articles...!

Excellent value at **£14.00**

(*Please add £1.00 for postage and packing*)

Please make cheques payable to "**Kevin O'Hagan**"
and post to
23 Chester road, Bristol BS5 7AX
Telephone: 0117-9525711
Genuine 60 minutes of action guaranteed
* Please mention where you saw this advert

Genuine 60 minutes of action guaranteed
IMPACT JUJUTSU Vol II

The follow on to 'Impact Jujutsu'

This time learn advanced drills, exercises and conditioning routines. Some unique to Kevin O'Hagan and his Ju Jutsu system.

See it all put together in Freestyle all out sparring too!

The new follow up video to the successful
IMPACT JUJUTSU Vol 1

This time **Kevin O'Hagan, 5th Dan Jujutsu,** and his senior instructor Paul Flett, take you through a full array of advanced exercises including:

Conditioning, Speed drills, Throws, Padwork, Groundwork drills, Boxing, Vale Tudo (Sparring) and much more…

This tape is a must for anybody serious about training for peak fitness and all round Cross training skills.

Enjoy and learn from this informative and exciting new video available **only** from Kevin O'Hagan.

Excellent value at **£14.00**
(*Please add £1.00 for postage and packing*)

Please make cheques payable to '**Kevin O'Hagan**'
and post to
23 Chester road, Bristol BS5 7AX
Telephone: 0117-9525711
* Please mention where you saw this advert

186

I THOUGHT
You'd be
BIGGER !

A SMALL PERSONS
guide to
FIGHTING BACK
by Kevin O'Hagan

**£ 14 inc Post and packing
from
New Breed, Po box 511
Dagenham, Essex RM9 5DN**

www.newbreedbooks.co.uk

A NEW BOOK

AVAILABLE NOW

BY
Kevin O'Hagan

£ 14 inc Post and packing
from
New Breed, Po box 511
Dagenham, Essex RM9 5DN

In Your Face
'CLOSE QUARTER FIGHTING'
by
Kevin O'Hagan

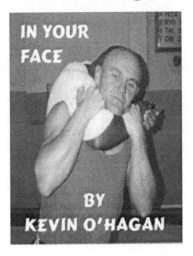

£ 14

from
£ 14 inc Post and packing
from
New Breed, Po box 511
Dagenham, Essex RM9 5DN

No One Fears When Angry
The Psychology of Confrontation
By Jamie O'Keefe
out now

THE GLORY BOYS

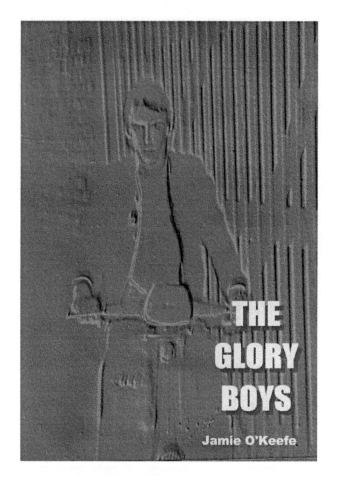

THE LONG AWAITED BOOK
For followers of the late 70s New Wave Mod Culture
'THE GLORY BOYS'
by Jamie O'Keefe
WILL BE RELEASED LATER IN 2002

www.newbreedbooks.co.uk

THE GLORY BOYS

This book covers the exploits of the 1977-79 Second Generation Mod explosion through the experiences of the notorious East London Gang 'The Glory Boys'

Jamie O'Keefe was a leading figure in this outfit of rebellious teenagers and tells the whole complete story of the fights, fun and fashion.

If you were connected in any way with the New Breed of mods that were around in the late 1970s or are interested in the how bands like 'The Jam, Secret affair, The Purple Hearts & The Chords' were connected with the Glory Boys, you will enjoy this book.

This is going to be the 'scoot culture' book of the century
Available December 2002 direct from

NEW BREED PUBLISHING
PO BOX 511
DAGENHAM
ESSEX RM9 5DN

@ £14 inc p&p

If you have purchased any book from New Breed, you will automatically be informed when it is available.

www.newbreedbooks.co.uk

The new Multimedia CD Rom from
MAD FRANKIE FRASER
That charts the life of one of Britain's
Most violent men

Telephone: **020 7837 5307**
www.madfrankiefraser.co.uk

WOMEN'S SELF DEFENCE COURSES

STREET CRIME IS ON THE INCREASE!
WORRIED ABOUT YOUR PERSONAL SAFETY?

COURSES IN LONDON

SUBJECTS COVERED

AWARENESS & AVOIDANCE
BODY LANGUAGE
VOICE CONTROL
FEAR CONTROL
EFFECTIVE STRIKES
EVERYDAY ITEMS AS WEAPONS
DEFENDING FROM THE FLOOR
THE LAW & SELF DEFENCE

FREE! PERSONAL ALARM WHEN YOU COMPLETE THE COURSE

DON'T BECOME A VICTIM!

To find out more contact your fully qualified instructor
LIZ CLARK *on: 07967 243 667*
E-mail: lizzie.clark@tesco.net

Log onto
WWW.WOMENS-SELFDEFENCE.CO.UK

The only U.K. Female Self Protection Coach approved
by Jamie O'Keefe

STREET COMBAT

GRAPPLING

VOLUME ONE (BASICS)

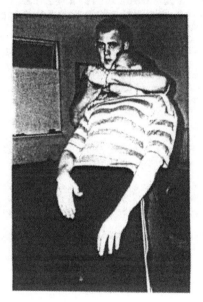

FIGHTING CHANCE
Books & Videos
For current price list and special offers
Tel: Dave Turton on 01709 710 489
Po Box 340, Rotherham, S62 6YL
* Please mention where you saw this advert

STREET COMBAT
GRAPPLING
VOLUME TWO (INTERMEDIATE)

STREET COMBAT
GRAPPLING
VOLUME THREE (ADVANCED)

LADIES'
SELF-DEFENCE

(VOLUME ONE)

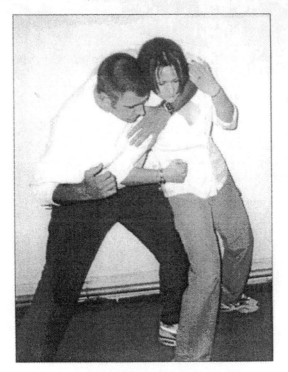

A FIGHTING CHANCE
PRODUCTION

SAFETY FIRST (UK)
Training Available
Our current list of training programmes and services:

Accredited Conflict Management & Personal Safety Training

Open College Network Accreditations

- *Introduction to Personal Safety - Level 1* *
- *Personal Safety - Self Protection - Level 2* *
- *Staff Personal Safety Awareness - Level 2* *
- *Conflict Management Instructor's Training - Level 3* *

Edexcel Foundation/BTEC Qualification

- *Conflict Management Instruction - BTEC Advanced Award* *

Additional 1 & 2 Days Short Courses

- *Recognition and Resolution of Conflict at Work*
- *Staff Personal Safety Awareness Training*
- *Personal Safety/Self Defence Training*
- *Stress Management & Relaxation*

Specialist Training & Services

- *Personal Security*
- *Control & Restraint Training*
- *Close Quarter Defence Techniques Training*

Available as Distance Learning Programmes

For further information regarding our training programmes or services, please contact:

Safety First (UK), 2 Lansdowne Row, Berkeley Square,
Mayfair, London, W1J 6HL.
E-mail: personalsafetyfirst@hotmail.com
Telephone: 0207 306 3399
© Safety First (UK)